THE SOLOMON PROMISE

THE KEY TO HEALING

AMERICA AND OURSELVES

HENRY BLACKABY

with RICHARD BLACKABY

W PUBLISHING GROUP

AN IMPRINT OF THOMAS NELSON

The Solomon Promise

© 2003, 2021 Henry Blackaby and Richard Blackaby

Portions of this book were originally published as *Holiness: God's Plan for Fullness of Life* © 2003 Henry Blackaby. Published by Thomas Nelson, Nashville, Tennessee. Thomas Nelson is a registered trademark of HarperCollins Christian Publishing, Inc.

Published in Nashville, Tennessee, by W Publishing, an imprint of Thomas Nelson.

Thomas Nelson titles may be purchased in bulk for educational, business, fundraising, or sales promotional use. For information, please e-mail SpecialMarkets@ThomasNelson.com.

Unless otherwise noted, Scripture quotations are taken from the New King James Version*. Copyright © 1982 by Thomas Nelson. Used by permission. All rights reserved.

Scripture quotations marked NIV are taken from The Holy Bible, New International Version*, NIV*. Copyright © 1973, 1978, 1984, 2011 by Biblica, Inc.* Used by permission of Zondervan. All rights reserved worldwide. www.Zondervan.com. The "NIV" and "New International Version" are trademarks registered in the United States Patent and Trademark Office by Biblica, Inc.*

Any internet addresses, phone numbers, or company or product information printed in this book are offered as a resource and are not intended in any way to be or to imply an endorsement by Thomas Nelson, nor does Thomas Nelson vouch for the existence, content, or services of these sites, phone numbers, companies, or products beyond the life of this book.

ISBN 978-0-7852-4936-8 (Jacketed Hardcover)
ISBN 978-0-7852-4937-5 (eBook)

Library of Congress Cataloging-in-Publication Data
Blackaby, Henry T., 1935–
    Holiness: God's plan for fullness of life / Henry Blackaby & Kerry Skinner.
    p. cm.
    ISBN 0-7852-6321-7
    1. Christian life. 2. Holiness—Christianity. I. Skinner, Kerry L., 1955–II. Title.
    BV4509.5.B546 2003
    234'.8—dc21   2003012108

Printed in the United States of America
21 22 23 24 25   LSC   10 9 8 7 6 5 4 3 2 1

To our fourteen grandchildren as they
faithfully pursue God's will in their lives

Mike, Daniel, Carrie, Erin, Matthew,
Conor, Christa, Stephen, Sarah, Emily,
Douglas, Anne, Elizabeth, and Joshua.

Contents

FOREWORD

THE CITY WAS ABUZZ. SOLOMON, THE CHOSEN HEIR OF King David, had finally completed his magnificent temple to Yahweh. No expense had been spared. Towering above Mount Moriah, it was the most magnificent building the people had ever seen. The king, in all his grandeur, consecrated the sacred structure to God, vowing he and his people would remain devoted to God. Suddenly, fire descended from heaven and consumed the burnt offerings. The glory of God filled the temple so powerfully that the priests dreaded entering it. Twenty-two thousand cattle and 120,000 sheep and goats were sacrificed in a spectacular offering to God. The Levites played musical instruments, the priests blew trumpets, and the people stood in awe. Worship lasted seven days.

No one present doubted they were witnessing the greatest days of their nation. The most powerful king in Israel's history was wholly dedicated to God. A spectacular temple and well-organized priesthood stood ready to help the people worship the one true God. It would have been utterly incomprehensible to imagine that succeeding generations would not embrace God and enjoy His bountiful blessings.

But ominous storm clouds were already gathering. Solomon, renowned for his wisdom, had utilized contemporary worldly reasoning. To ensure peace for his kingdom, he had married hundreds of princesses from the neighboring nations. He then built temples for his wives' gods (1 Kings 11:1–8). These temples were typically built on high places, such as hilltops, that had once been centers of Canaanite pagan worship. By mixing the world's ways with God's, Solomon planted the seeds of his people's apostasy and ultimate destruction. For four centuries, God sent prophets denouncing the pagan worship to no avail. Ultimately, God dispatched Nebuchadnezzar and his Babylonian hordes in 586 B.C. to decimate Jerusalem's defenses and level Solomon's beautiful temple. Seventy years later, God's people returned to Jerusalem and vowed to walk loyally with Him. But, once again, they forsook Him to follow a religion of their own making. After repeated warnings over five centuries, Roman legions eventually appeared before Jerusalem's walls and obliterated the city and the new temple. Two thousand years later, Muslims worship Allah on the spot where God's glory once filled the temple. Scripture and history demonstrate that regardless of how fervently God's people worship Him, they inevitably depart from Him and face the dire consequences of apostasy.

Frail, sinful, foolish, prideful people cannot properly relate for long to an almighty, holy God. No matter how sincere their intentions, they inevitably fall short.

The current spiritual condition of America clearly shows that, just like ancient Israel, the nation has struggled to follow God's ways, abide by His word, and embrace His values. God has clearly blessed the United States. It is arguably the most prosperous, powerful nation in history. But whatever Christian principles originally undergirded its founding have largely been discarded. Postmodernism is today's pervading worldview. It postulates that there is no such thing as absolute truth (of that, postmodernists are absolutely certain!). People do what is right in their own eyes. Moral standards have plummeted to unprecedented depths. Though society is prosperous, depression and suicide are widespread among today's youth. Society

> Frail, sinful, foolish, prideful people cannot properly relate for long to an almighty, holy God.

is polarized. Racial issues plague the nation. Many leading voices today denounce Christianity's influence on culture, but their modern alternatives only make matters worse.

One would think this current climate is a perfect opportunity for the church to demonstrate the wisdom of drawing near to God and embracing His ways. Yet the church is in trouble. Roughly 70% of today's churches are plateaued or in decline, around 4,000 churches disband each year, and 67% of people who regularly attended church as teenagers are abandoning Christianity before they graduate from college. The fastest growing religious group in America today is the "Nones," who claim to have no religion whatsoever. America has seemingly entered a death spiral from which it cannot escape.

But there is one ray of hope. Shortly after Solomon dedicated the temple, God made a promise that seemed unnecessary at the time. After the nation had dedicated itself to serve the Lord, God revealed that He knew their loyalty was fleeting. God said when they forsook Him, not if, He would summon enemies, drought, pestilence, and plagues against them. God would allow circumstances to deteriorate until the people were so desperate they were ready to return to Him. When they reached that point, God promised, "If My people, who bear My name, humble themselves, pray and seek My face, and turn from their evil ways, then I will hear from heaven, forgive their sin, and heal their land" (2 Chr. 7:14).

Some people are quick to interject that this covenant was made to the nation of Israel under the old covenant, which is true. Context is important. But some things never change. God is the same today as He has always been (Mal. 3:16). Likewise, people are as sinful and prone to depart from Him today as they have always been. And, perhaps most importantly, the principle "as go God's people, so goes the nation" remains as applicable today as it has been to every previous generation. So God's people would be wise to examine the promise God made to Solomon. It is our only hope.

I am encouraged that my father's classic work is being re-released. This material stems from my father's sermons, not academic lectures on the theory of revival. They emanated from his personal experience. I heard him deliver these sermons. Had you been in the auditorium as he spoke, you would have found yourself on your face at the altar. As my father preached, people wept in prayer. I saw grown men lying prostrate on the floor, heaving with sobs as they

> God's people would be wise to examine the promise God made to Solomon. It is our only hope.

lay exposed and broken before a holy God. I doubt written words can fully capture the feeling people experienced when the Holy Spirit gripped their hearts and assured them the message my father preached was absolutely true.

Society doesn't need a new, psychologically improved solution for its ills. It doesn't require sterilized, politically correct answers that are grounded in nothing more than popular opinion. Society desperately needs timeless answers from God that work just as powerfully today as they have in every previous age. It is time to return to the Solomon Promise to see if God will do once again what he promised 3,000 years ago.

As you read this book, pray and prepare your heart so you don't merely encounter a book or an author but the author's God. Don't rush through the pages. Some of what you read might disturb or offend you. The message is direct and hard-hitting. But it is true. Set aside any preconceived ideas of God's character and ways and allow Him to express Himself to you as He actually is. Then be prepared to never be the same again.

Richard Blackaby
President, Blackaby
Ministries International

INTRODUCTION

THESE MESSAGES ARE AT THE HEART OF MY LIFE AND ministry. Preached in one form or another, these truths have developed in my life over many years. They are my life-messages to God's people, as God calls us to renewal, revival, and spiritual awakening. These truths first began to make a deep impression on my life when I was a young boy. I remember listening to my layman father teach and preach. He began a church in a dance hall in a violent, sinful city on the northern coast of British Columbia, Canada. He encountered many broken lives in that alcohol-soaked city. He wept before the Lord over the condition of the people. Time and again he preached passionately on sin, repentance, the fear of God, and holiness. At times the sin in the lives of desperate people overwhelmed him as he sought to live out his Christian life with integrity. He remained faithful in his personal holiness. Our family also lived our lives under the deep conviction of the return of the Lord and its accompanying accountability. All this left a deep impression on my young life.

As a young man my life and message were also shaped toward repentance and revival through the many stories and pictures my family received from China during the great Shantung Revival. My aunt and uncle were missionaries in China during those awesome and exciting times when God moved mightily after His people began taking His holiness seriously.

During the early days of my ministry God convinced me of His holiness and the need for His people to return to Him. God used the writings of Oswald Chambers and Duncan Campbell to impact me deeply. The year before I went to Faith Baptist Church in Saskatoon to become their pastor, Duncan Campbell had been in the city. He left a significant mark on the city and indicated that he believed God would send revival to Canada and that it would begin in Saskatoon. This promise of revival and the witness of his godly life were some of the reasons I accepted the call to that church.

I had already felt the weight of sin and the deep need for biblical repentance while pastoring in California. I trembled before God as I realized that many of God's people no longer feared God or sin, and no longer pursued holiness. As a pastor I saw the consequences of sin in God's people. I preached passionately and taught God's people to fear God, hate sin, thoroughly repent before holy God, and to seek holiness as a lifestyle.

God honored the fervent and faithful proclamation of these truths to His people. God's people did heed God's word, and lives and families were dramatically transformed. The communities where I pastored were changed in numerous ways, and many souls were saved. God graciously granted me the privilege of experiencing touches of genuine revival. My first encounter with deep and powerful revival was in Saskatoon, Saskatchewan in western Canada. After I had spent much time in prayer with other pastors, God suddenly moved mightily, every night, for seven weeks! Churches were deeply impacted, and thousands of lives were changed. The effects of those days are still being felt decades later. During this time, we saw many people saved, new churches started, and numerous people called into the ministry. Many churches experienced great renewal.

Later, at Howard Payne University in Texas, God allowed me to see and experience revival with the people there. This revival affected hundreds of other colleges and many seminary campuses. The truths God had burned into my heart were being confirmed in changed lives. Again, in Ft. Collins, Colorado, I witnessed twenty-one straight hours of deep brokenness and repentance in a gathering of several thousand Campus Crusade workers. I regularly encounter many of those changed lives as I travel all over the world. In addition, I have witnessed the powerful stirring of the Holy Spirit in countless church services and conferences where altars were filled, people lingered for hours to weep and pray, and lives were dramatically transformed. I have had people stream to the altar in the middle of my sermon to get right with God, and I have watched men and women lying prostrate on the floor weeping before holy God.

My life has been shaped by God through these experiences of revival and renewal, and thus the heart messages of my ministry have been greatly deepened. In this book I share what God has placed on my heart for His people. Today, I am passionately burdened to share these much-needed truths with God's people:

- The loss of the *fear* of God

- Seeing *sin* from God's perspective

- The *highway of holiness*

Introduction

May God graciously grant that these words and truths continue to draw God's people toward Him and thus toward the experience of deep revival. My life-message continues to be toward revival and spiritual awakening in this nation and across the world—for the glory of God!

Chapter 1

THE LOSS OF THE FEAR OF GOD

IT IS THE PEOPLE OF GOD WHO CAN TRULY SHAPE A NATION. Many look to political or economic leaders or cultural icons to solve a nation's problems. But generally, politicians and governments cannot restore a nation once it is on a downward slide. While leaders and governments can influence a nation, there is no group of people who can determine the future of a nation like God's people.

As go the people of God, so goes the redemption of the world. God is therefore working mightily among His own. We are closer to either revival or judgment than we have ever been. There is no alternative between these two. Either God's people return to Him with all of their hearts, or God will judge our nation. We do not have to guess how

> As go the people of God, so goes the redemption of the world.

that judgment will look or how thorough it will be. The Bible indicates how God judges His people. Any nation that turns away from God comes under His judgment. When God judged the Northern Kingdom of Israel, He annihilated them. When God judged Judah, the Southern Kingdom, He destroyed Jerusalem, decimated the temple, and exiled the people for seventy years. God also took the people in Jesus' day and scattered them so thoroughly that they did not join together as a nation again for nineteen hundred years, just as Jesus predicted.

If we look at the history of God's dealings with His people it ought to cause us to tremble. But it is the loss of the fear of God that characterizes God's people in America today.

DEFINING REVIVAL

In 1987 there was a conference on prayer and spiritual awakening in North Carolina. The keynote speaker, Dr. J. Edwin Orr, spoke on April 21. His message was *Revival Is Like Judgment Day*. That was the last message he ever preached. The next day he passed away and went to meet his Lord whom he had served so faithfully. That message has stayed on my heart to this day. The topic of that sermon is consistent with the Scripture—*revival is like judgment day.*

But many of us are not thinking about judgment; we are thinking about revival. We have redefined revival in our day as something different from how Scripture defines it. We have adjusted the definition to be more palatable to our tastes. We have changed God into our image. We have transformed worship, youth work, and family life to be what we want. We have altered, for application in our own lives, nearly every commandment of God. We continue to break the Ten Commandments. If I were to take you through what the Scripture says about the Sabbath day, you would see that God's people have utterly desecrated it—that is, if you take the Scripture as the guideline for how to act on the Sabbath day. But as long as people do what is right in their own eyes and everyone else is doing the same thing, we assume that as long as God does not judge us, everything is okay. But it is not. Today, there is an incredible heart cry for revival. I think it is a God-created hunger. I think it is a cry to God that exclaims, *Oh, God, revive us again so that Your people may rejoice in You!* I want you to understand the nature of what God is doing.

I assume as you consider this message that you have a

> Our nation, our churches, and our families need a deep personal encounter with God.

heart cry for revival. But understand that our nation, our churches, and our families need a deep personal encounter with God. We must be reoriented back to God at every level of life. That heart cry in your life is real and personal, but your involvement in God's activity does not come simply because you listen to a message. It comes from a deep personal and corporate processing. When you hear the Word of God, it immediately begins a process in you to understand and respond to what He is saying. When you come face to face with God and He says something through His Word, the Holy Spirit helps you to realize the urgency of your response. *If this is what God says, then this is what I must do, immediately.*

BLESSING OR CURSE

Remember when the priests were cleaning the temple in Josiah's day and they found the Scriptures? The Bible says, "Now it happened, when the king heard the words of the Book of the Law, that he tore his clothes" (2 Kings 22:11).

Do you recall when the priests took those Scriptures and began to read them in the presence of the king? You can find the entire story in 2 Kings 22 and 23. Suddenly the king realized for the first time what the standard had been all along and that God is not mocked. Whatever a people sow, they will reap. The king was no longer ignorant of what that would look like, because now the covenant was being read concerning what God would do *if* the people followed and practiced what God said. In Deuteronomy 28 and Leviticus 23, the covenant listed all God expected His people to do. The first part of the covenant was very positive.

The negative side of the covenant began with Deuteronomy 28:15. God said that if they did not obey His commands, then He would reverse all their blessings as a covenant people of God—chosen, encountered, instructed, and separated by Him. God listed in Deuteronomy 28:15–68 the awful things that would happen to His people if they refused to follow Him. Verse fifteen is the dreadful beginning of those words:

> But it shall come to pass, if you do not obey the voice of the LORD your God, to observe carefully all His commandments and His statutes which I command you today, that all these curses will come upon you and overtake you.
>
> DEUTERONOMY 28:15

When Josiah heard that, he trembled. The Spirit of God, who was upon him to enable him to function as king, pierced his heart. The king immediately began to weep and tear his clothes. He put on sackcloth and ashes and called for the people to repent. Josiah realized that God meant what He said. He understood there were no exceptions. He realized they were standing on the edge of destruction.

The problem was that the priests had set the Scriptures aside so the people no longer knew what they said. They were covered with debris. All the time the Scriptures were being ignored, judgment was approaching. The nation was rapidly proceeding toward God's judgment because it had lost its standard. The people had nothing to guide them. So, they would sit and discuss what they thought was acceptable to God. But it did not matter what they thought, it was what God had said that was important. Everyone was doing what was right in their own eyes, moving steadily toward the devastating judgment of God. Judgment was nigh. Josiah wisely understood the dire condition of the nation. He immediately adjusted his life to God. The king commanded the spiritual leaders to quickly summon the people to repent corporately (2 Kings 22:11–23:3).

God listened to Josiah's heart and sent word to him:

"Because your heart was tender, and you humbled yourself before the LORD when you heard what I spoke against this place and against its inhabitants, that they would become a desolation and a curse, and you tore your clothes and wept before Me, I also have heard you," says the LORD. "Surely, therefore, I will gather you to your fathers, and you shall be gathered to your grave in peace; and your eyes shall not see all the calamity which I will bring on this place."

2 KINGS 22:19–20

What happens when you come face to face with the Word of God? Do you tremble when God speaks? Isaiah 66:2 says, "But on this one will I look: on him who is poor and of a contrite spirit, and who trembles at My word." When was the last time you were confronted by God in His Word and you shook like a leaf?

FEAR OF GOD/FEAR OF SIN

I made a phone call recently to a significant leader of an organization, who told me, "Henry, I am so grateful that you called. You have no idea the importance of this phone call." I had made a covenant with him to call him on a regular basis because his position of leadership was extremely influential. When I asked him what was happening, he said, "Never in my life have I been so utterly terrified. God has chosen to deal with the sin in my life. He has brought up things that I have not thought about for many years. He has reminded me of things from my youth that I have never dealt with—issues that have affected my marriage and my work. God was relentless for three weeks bringing to mind what He sees as sin and impressing on me how serious it is with Him. I came to the place a few days ago where I cried out to God and asked why God was doing this to me. God said, 'I am doing this because you have lost the fear of Me.'"

When you do not fear God, you will not fear sin. There is a direct relationship between a high view of God and a high view of sin. A low view of God brings a low view of sin. When there is no fear of God, there is no fear of sin. It is amazing to me the number of people who sin grievously against the Word of God. In the Old Testament, they would have been put to death for many of the things people do today. In fact, the New Testament takes sin far more seriously than the Old Testament. It amazes me how so many people believe that as long as they do not feel that something is bad, then it can't be wrong—as long as they feel okay about it, they can continue doing it. As long as God does not deal with them immediately, it must not be sin. We are moving ever closer to a devastating confrontation with a holy God who makes no exceptions.

This man I had called said, "Henry, I want you to know that only in the last three weeks has God put on my heart an understanding of why we do not see revival. We do not see the hand of God moving on the people of God because we have lost the fear of God."

> We are moving ever closer to a devastating confrontation with a holy God who makes no exceptions.

Later, I was in another state talking with a large group of people. Several came up to talk with me after the meeting and told me what was happening in their church. They said that the church had taken a vote to begin a building program. The constitution of the church stated they must have a 75 percent vote to proceed. They had a 72 percent vote. They said the pastor had thrown a fit and began to berate the people. He took 100 of the church members and was looking for a building to start another church a mile down the street.

When I heard that, I began to tremble. The Scripture

warns that you cannot harm the body of Christ without God dealing with you severely (Acts 5:1–5).

I have listened to story after story of people who have suffered through church splits all over this nation. The people responsible for them do not have a fear of God at all! They tend to comment that at least they started another church. They did not start a church—they started a religious club! God did not have anything to do with the split. The Spirit of God is never involved in a church split. Never! He is the author of unity. God's people can explain it away all they want so they feel good about it. But when you have a church split, you cancel your right to preach the gospel of reconciliation (2 Cor. 5:18–19). That church just demonstrated that the God who reconciles sinners to Himself cannot reconcile His own people with one another. What message does that present to the world? The tragedy is that there is no fear of God.

During thirty years of pastoring, I witnessed how our sin wreaks havoc on our children. When we claim to be Christians but refuse to repent of our sin, our children grow up and want nothing to do with the people of God. They marry non-Christian spouses and later divorce. Our grandchildren suffer because of our sin, and another Christian heritage comes to an end. Some say God did not judge them. You do not understand—He just did! God said the hearts of your children will be turned away from Him—they will not follow in His ways.

Marilyn and I have prayed from the moment our first child was born, Oh, God, keep us holy, for the sake of our children. Keep us walking with You. Use us to love and build up the people of God so our children will want to serve You and be active in church too.

My heart cry is for me and the people of God around me to come back to God's Word and to let Him tell us what His standard is so we can live by it.

RETURNING TO GOD

The term *revive* means "to return the life to." Lost people cannot be revived because they never had life in the first place. They first have to be saved—awakened to their lost condition. Revival is exclusively what God does to His people. When the life of God has departed from the people of God and they are content to live without the manifest presence of God—content week after week without any evidence of the presence and power of God—then they need to be revived. They need the life of God to return to them.

I want to give you a word picture of what it is like when the presence of God falls on His people. Have you ever been in the midst of anything like this, or is this what you have imagined from the Scripture that revival would be like?

> "Behold, I send My messenger,
> And he will prepare the way before Me.
> And the Lord, whom you seek,
> Will suddenly come to His temple,
> Even the Messenger of the covenant,
> In whom you delight.
> Behold, He is coming,"
> Says the LORD of hosts.

> "But who can endure the day of His coming?
> And who can stand when He appears?
> For He is like a refiner's fire
> And like launderers' soap.
> He will sit as a refiner and a purifier of silver;
> He will purify the sons of Levi,
> And purge them as gold and silver,
> That they may offer to the LORD
> An offering in righteousness.

The Loss of the Fear of God

"Then the offering of Judah and Jerusalem
Will be pleasant to the LORD,
As in the days of old,
As in former years.
And I will come near you for judgment;
I will be a swift witness
Against sorcerers,
Against adulterers,
Against perjurers,
Against those who exploit wage earners and widows
and orphans,
And against those who turn away an alien—
Because they do not fear Me,"
Says the LORD of hosts.

MALACHI 3:1–5

I was aware of a situation not long ago in which it was discovered that a pastor had rented motel rooms so he could commit adultery with a woman. No one had known about it. But that really was not true. God was there when the pastor checked in to the motel! When God deals with him, He will testify against him. That should cause us to tremble! Things we have long hidden from the eyes of others were not done in secret from God. In revival, God is the chief witness against us.

If you lose the fear of God, there is nothing to restrain you from sin. Many do not believe God sees them and do not think He is aware of the condition of their hearts. They assume that if He sees them and does not stop them, then it must be okay. But He does see you! He may not stop you immediately, but it is *not* okay. If the Word of God says it is sin, then it is sin.

> "For I am the LORD, I do not change;
> Therefore you are not consumed, O sons of Jacob.
> Yet from the days of your fathers
> You have gone away from My ordinances
> And have not kept them.
> Return to Me, and I will return to you,"
> Says the LORD of hosts.
> "But you said,
> 'In what way shall we return?'"
>
> MALACHI 3:6–7

When we hear a message that calls us to return to the Lord, God's people consistently say, Well, wherein do I need to return? I am a Christian. I have been born again.

I was baptized. I am a leader in the church. I am going to heaven when I die. What do you mean, "return to God"?

If there is any area where God's people are disoriented in their walk with God, it is in the matter of repentance. If a pastor were to preach a sermon on repentance, many church members would bow their heads and pray, *Oh, God, if there is any lost person here, I pray that they will hear this word and repent.* But God is shouting at His people saying, *It is not only the lost who need to repent—it is God's people who need to repent!* We are the ones who have moved away from the Lord.

So, with a compassionate and deeply concerned heart, God came and told the prophet Malachi to say to His people that the God whom they had been seeking would suddenly come to His temple (Mal. 3:1). When He comes in our day, no one will be able to speak except God. When God is through speaking, you will know what He thinks about what you have done.

> God is shouting at His people saying, *It is not only the lost who need to repent—it is God's people who need to repent!* We are the ones who have moved away from the Lord.

Chapter 2

LOOKING AT SIN FROM GOD'S PERSPECTIVE

GOD IS CALLING HIS PEOPLE TO RETURN TO HIM AND BE a *highway of holiness* over which He comes to the lost world. But before we can become a highway of holiness, we must understand the issue of sin. In order to understand sin, we must see our sin from God's perspective. We must develop our relationship with God in such a way that our lives become a highway over which God reaches the rest of our nation. God wants to ignite a great revival among His people that leads to a sweeping spiritual awakening in the hearts and lives of those who do not know Him.

God is generating a sense of urgency among his people. There are at least two aspects to this. The first has to do with the relationship between prayer and revival. The second deals with repentance and God's judgment. If I understand the Scriptures correctly, God will judge any nation that neglects His direction. It may well be that we are already under the judgment of God.

If I were to attempt to identify the beginning of what I believe is a national neglect of God, I would turn to the early 1960s. It seems as though God removed the hedge of protection from around America in that decade (Is. 5:1–7). We began to see unrestrained sin and debauchery take place from the '60s to the present day. There seems to have been little to hold back the tide of injustice in society. A deep departure from God in the churches has continued since that decade. It is as if the hedge of His protection has been broken down, and God is letting us experience the awful consequences of our sin.

The salvation of the nation has little to do with Washington or Hollywood—it has everything to do with the people of God!

There is an urgency in the Scriptures when God says, "If My people who are called by My name will humble themselves, and pray and seek My face, and turn from their wicked ways, then I will hear from heaven, and will forgive their sin and heal their land" (2 Chron. 7:14). That great passage clearly indicates that the redemption of America waits on the repentance of God's people. The salvation of the nation has little to do with Washington or Hollywood—it has everything to do with the people of God! If God's people do not sense that the problem is with them, then America does not stand a chance of revival or survival. And so, understanding in ever-increasing measure what God says in His Word, we carry with us a deep sense of urgency that we are closer to the judgment of God on our nation today than we have ever been before.

REVIVAL AND PRAYER

Do you believe that when God's people pray, God hears, responds, and brings about deep change? Are you helping your family and the people in your church to pray for the condition of their lives, families, church, and nation? Remember, God declared, "For the eyes of the LORD run to and fro throughout the whole earth, to show Himself strong on behalf of those whose heart is loyal to Him" (2 Chron. 16:9). He also said, "The effective, fervent prayer of a righteous man avails much" (James 5:16). Jesus promised, "And whatever you ask in My name [consistent with everything I have taught you], that I will do, that the Father may be glorified in the Son" (John 14:13). With these promises available to you—with which God's people can change the course of a nation's history—what are your prayers like for your own life, your marriage, your family, your church, and your nation?

If revival in America depended on your prayer life, would there be a revival? If you have to say, *Not my prayer life,* then you must change your prayer life. To have a renewed prayer life is a simple matter of personal choice. Your life is the product of choices you have made, and your church is the product of choices it has made. Your church's corporate prayer meeting is a reflection of the choices you have made as a church. Your nation is a reflection of the choices your church has made concerning its relationship with God.

That is one of the reasons why this message has an urgency to it. There is an enormous amount at stake. In fact, eternity is in question for many in our nation. However, in your church alone, there are enough of God's people—if they were serious with God—to turn the course of the nation back to Him.

There were only 120 people in the upper room who were wholly yielded to the person of Jesus Christ (Acts 1:15). God used them to turn the entire Roman empire upside down. In 1904 God used a young man from Wales named Evan Roberts. God broke him and shook him through a specific time of prayer—with others who had been praying across the land—and 100,000 people came to faith in Jesus Christ in six months. The great revival of 1904–1905 began with prayer. Thousands of people ended up on the mission field as a result. Roberts, at twenty-six, was focused on prayer and revival, and that revival set in motion a great missionary movement.

> In your church alone, there are enough of God's people—if they were serious with God—to turn the course of our nation back to Him.

What could God do through your life? Do you sense that America needs a mighty touch of God? Do you believe God could work through your life as He has done with others throughout history? Would you be willing to make the kind of choices required by God to be that kind of person? Your response to this message will reflect the choices you have made concerning your Lord.

URGENCY OF THE HOUR

There is another reason why there is such urgency for God's people to be completely yielded to Him today. I believe this may be the generation that is still living when the Lord Jesus returns. I believe that God may now be calling the last generation of those who will go with Him on mission to the ends of the earth. Most of the leaders I have encountered in the last few years—whether a pastor of a local church, a leader of a ministry group, or a leader of a denomination—have earnestly told me that they believe with all their hearts that we may be the generation that is still living when the Lord Jesus comes back.

Do you suppose, since the Father knows the time, the day, and the hour when He will say, *Enough—time shall be no more. My Son will come in the clouds, judgment will begin, and eternity will be ushered in,* He could be causing an urgency in the hearts of His people and His churches, knowing that the hour is short and there is limited time for people to respond? Do you believe we will face our Lord and give an account to Him for the way in which we have lived (2 Cor. 5:10)? Do you suppose if our Father knows the time of His coming that He may have already issued the instruction to the Spirit of God to make His followers aware of the need to repent, as if to say:

Make My people understand the urgency of the hour, that when they hear My Word, there will be an intense

urgency in their hearts. Cause My people to understand that to invest their lives in the world that will
pass away is not as important as investing their lives in
the kingdom that will never pass away.

God is stirring the hearts of children, young people,
college students, those in midcareer, and even retired
people with a call to missions as never before. Recently, a
very large international missions agency told me they had
processed a record number of people who were inquiring
about the pursuit of international mission appointments.
Did you know that just a few years ago, in one year, one
denomination had over 300,000 people volunteer for mission projects in North America and internationally? They
anticipate seeing 500,000 from their churches going on
mission to the ends of the earth.

In recent times many have said, "In an amazing way,
over the last several years, God has stirred my heart and
caused me to go on a mission trip. I never dreamed I would
be serving in another part of the world, but something
happened in my heart, and I went, and I have never been
the same." This stirring in the hearts of volunteers is happening among the people of God all over the world. I do
not believe this is accidental. This is inspired by God, and

I believe it has something to do with the near return of our Lord. Because of these urgent times we must stand before God and His Word and see things from His perspective.

FROM THE HEAD TO THE HEART

It is not enough for God to speak to you from His Word, because all the head knowledge in the world will never change your life. However, when what you know in your head hits your heart, you will not be able to rest day or night until what you see in your Bible is also what you see in your life.

> All the truth believed in a person's head is also believed by the demons in hell, yet they are one step ahead of us.

I hear many people say, "Well, I believe Jesus is the Son of God. I believe He is the world's Savior." Much of the truth believed in a person's head is also believed by the demons, yet they are one step ahead of us. At least when they know the truth in their heads, they *tremble*. They know Jesus died for the sins of the world. They know He was the sinless Son of God. They know He was raised again. They know the power that raised Jesus from the dead has been given to every one of us who believes. They know He is interceding. They know He is coming back. There is not a truth you and I believe in our heads about God that they do not believe, and tremble. But the difference between the demons and us is that when we take it from our heads and let it impact our hearts, we cannot rest night or day until what God shows us in His Word is being lived out in our lives.

Second Corinthians 1:20 has made an incredible impact on my life. The passage says, "For all the promises of God in Him are Yes, and in Him Amen, to the glory of God through us." The moment you became united with Jesus Christ in the saving work of God through the death of His Son on the cross, every promise God ever made in the Bible has become *yes* for you. Now, many of you know that in your head, but let me tell you how to know if it has ever entered your heart. The moment you know that promise is true, it ought to be an obsession with you to find every promise God has ever given and live it out, so God can be that way in your life. If it is in your head only, it will not change anything in your life. But when you hear the blessed Lord Jesus say, "Most assuredly, I say to you, he who believes in Me, the works that I do he will do also; and *greater works* than these he will do, because I go to

My Father" (John 14:12, emphasis added), and that truth enters your heart, your life will never be the same again.

Can you imagine how dramatically the nation would be impacted if we believed just that one promise with all of our hearts? And there are hundreds of promises given in God's Word. Are you letting what you hear in your head go eighteen inches lower to your heart, and begin to change the way you live?

You and I have the enormous opportunity to make a difference because God has given us His promises. God says He will act when we respond: "Draw near to God and He will draw near to you" (James 4:8). Then why do we not draw near to God, and keep going in that direction until we know God has drawn near to us and His presence has changed everything about us? You cannot be in the presence of God and remain the same. That would be absolutely impossible. The Scripture, "Draw near to God and He will draw near to you," is straightforward, yet deeply profound.

Are you taking the promises of God and standing before Him until He is working in your life exactly as He promised He would? The tragedy is that many of God's people can know they are living their lives the same as the world around them without it disturbing them in the slightest. Did you know that it deeply disturbs God for us to live our way instead of His way? For God's people to go their own way is called sin. The Scripture says, "Whatever is not from faith is sin" (Rom. 14:23). The Scripture further explains, "Therefore, to him who knows to do good and does not do it, to him it is sin" (James 4:17). Another Scripture states, "Whoever commits sin also commits lawlessness, and sin is lawlessness" (1 John 3:4). One of the laws is that you, "Bear one another's burdens, and so fulfill the law of Christ" (Gal. 6:2). Sin is when you see a fellow Christian struggling with a burden, and you do not help carry it—that is sin, and that grieves God's heart.

There is nothing I see in the Scripture that burdens the heart of God more deeply than sin in the hearts and lives of His people. So, I want us to look at sin from God's perspective—not from ours. How does God view sin? Scripture says sin is coming short of what God requires. "Oh," you may say, "I'm just human." No, you are not; you are indwelt by almighty God if you have been born again!

You used to be just human, but now you are a child of the King of kings, indwelt as a temple of God,

> You used to be just human, but now you are a child of the King of kings.

and now your life is not yours—it is Christ living out His life in you. Is that not what Paul said? "I have been crucified with Christ; it is no longer I who live, but Christ lives in me; and the life which I now live in the flesh I live by faith in the Son of God, who loved me and gave Himself for me" (Gal. 2:20). That is not a figure of speech—that is a fact! For me to know that and to resist Him is sin. A definition of sin in 1 John 3:4 is that "sin is lawlessness [rebellion]." Rebellion is when you know what God says and yet you choose to disobey. I have often said the two words that cannot go together are *No, Lord.* One of those words has to be removed. If He is Lord, there is no possibility of you saying *no*. You cannot call Him *Lord* without also saying *yes*. What God is looking for are children who constantly say, "Yes, Lord."

SIN FROM MAN'S PERSPECTIVE

There is no greater prerequisite to revival than for us to see our sin from God's perspective and to deal with it immediately. I believe I could safely say there is no stronger passage in the Bible to which we could turn and see sin from people's perspective than Psalm 51:

Looking at Sin from God's Perspective

Have mercy upon me, O God,
According to Your lovingkindness;
According to the multitude of Your tender mercies,
Blot out my transgressions.
Wash me thoroughly from my iniquity,
And cleanse me from my sin.

For I acknowledge my transgressions,
And my sin is always before me.
Against You, You only, have I sinned,
And done this evil in Your sight—
That You may be found just when You speak,
And blameless when You judge.

Behold, I was brought forth in iniquity,
And in sin my mother conceived me.
Behold, You desire truth in the inward parts,
And in the hidden part You will make me to know
    wisdom.

Purge me with hyssop, and I shall be clean;
Wash me, and I shall be whiter than snow.
Make me hear joy and gladness,
That the bones You have broken may rejoice.

Hide Your face from my sins,
And blot out all my iniquities.

Create in me a clean heart, O God,
And renew a steadfast spirit within me.
Do not cast me away from Your presence,
And do not take Your Holy Spirit from me.

Restore to me the joy of Your salvation,
And uphold me by Your generous Spirit.
Then I will teach transgressors Your ways,
And sinners shall be converted to You.

Deliver me from the guilt of bloodshed, O God,
The God of my salvation,
And my tongue shall sing aloud of Your righteousness.
O Lord, open my lips,
And my mouth shall show forth Your praise.
For You do not desire sacrifice, or else I would
        give it;
You do not delight in burnt offering.
The sacrifices of God are a broken spirit,
A broken and a contrite heart—
These, O God, You will not despise.

Do good in Your good pleasure to Zion;
Build the walls of Jerusalem.
Then You shall be pleased with the sacrifices of
    righteousness,
With burnt offering and whole burnt offering;
Then they shall offer bulls on Your altar.

This psalm gives us a brief look at how David saw his sin. But you will never understand Psalm 51 unless you first see how God caused David to see his sin from God's perspective. God's viewpoint was far different from David's.

God made David aware of his sin. David would never have acknowledged his transgressions had God not granted him the understanding of them. God grants repentance. There have been many times when I have cried out, "Oh, God, would You grant Your people the capacity to understand and repent? If You do not move us toward repentance, we will continue in our own way. If You do not intervene in our lives, we will persist in our sin."

Psalm 51 was David's response to God's helping him realize that his sin was far more serious than David understood. This passage deals with his sin against Bathsheba and against Uriah, her husband (2 Sam. 11:3–26;12:9–10).

But you need to remember, when God sent Nathan to bring conviction to David's heart, it was probably a full year after David had committed his crime. The child from his sin of adultery had already been born when Nathan the prophet approached David. David had rationalized how to deal with his sin against Bathsheba. He had worked out a scheme by which he could kill Bathsheba's husband in war and then after a normal period of mourning, take her as one of his wives. It was only after David's yearlong cover-up that God finally sent Nathan to say, "David, you are the man!" (2 Sam. 12:7). God gave David more than a year to repent, but he did not. If God had not intervened, David probably never would have acknowledged his sin.

Yet God knew the essence of David's heart. God seemed to say, "David has a heart for me. Sin has blinded him—sin has distorted his reasoning. Sin has done what it always does. But I know David's heart, and if I confront David with his sin and I bring conviction to him about his sin, he will repent and return to Me, and he will be the person I know he can be."

But hear the cry of David. He says, "Have mercy upon me, O God" (Ps. 51:1). This passage gives you a thorough picture of genuine repentance.

What is mercy? When David said, "Have mercy upon

me, O God, according to Your lovingkindness; according to the multitude of Your tender mercies" (Ps. 51:1), he knew God would deal with his sin. What is your definition of mercy? Well, my understanding of mercy is that God withholds from me what I justly deserve. Mercy is God's withholding of what He has a right to do immediately. Would you want God to give you what you justly deserve?

What did David deserve from God? Death. He had committed adultery and murder. His sin called for immediate death. When we turn to another passage, we see that God granted David mercy. Nathan said to David, "The LORD also has put away your sin; you shall not die" (2 Sam. 12:13). It is as though Nathan said, "God has forgiven your sin, and you will not die. David, you could have died. God would have been absolutely just in punishing you severely. David, you have got to see your sin from God's perspective."

> Mercy is God's withholding what He has a right to do immediately. Would you want God to give you what you justly deserve?

The first cry of David was, "Have mercy upon me, O God!" As David continued his thoughts through the psalm, he used a number of different terms. He said, "Blot out my transgressions" (Ps. 51:1). I can almost hear David say, "Lord, I violated your clear guidelines. You said, 'Do not commit adultery,' and I did. "You said. 'Thou shalt not kill,' but I did." It was specific in Your Word, and I violated it. Oh, Lord, would You blot out my transgressions?" If God did not deal with David's sin, it was all over for David. He had violated clear commands of God.

God is not merely a loving Father in the heavens; He is a righteous, holy God. Every time His children violate something He has said, it reflects on God's holy name. It empties God's name of its holiness and righteousness.

One of the great deterrents from going astray when I was a young man was my dear father who was a deacon and a godly layman. He led more people to Jesus than any other person I have known, including myself. He worked in the business world, but he was one of the most faithful Christians I ever knew. I watched my dad pay a price for integrity and righteousness in the business world.

One day my dad came to me and my two brothers and said, "Boys, I want you to know that I have spent a lifetime building meaning and value into my name, and wherever you go, you take my name with you. It has cost me my life to put integrity into my name; now you carry my name with you." When I was tempted to sin and could have gone astray, I remembered my dad, and I thought, *I couldn't do that to him. I carry his name, and my dad has a reputation as a godly Christian businessman. I couldn't do that to him.*

For me to sin without regard to the name I carry would be to bring the deepest pain to my father possible, for he sought to honor his Lord by the way he lived. He entrusted his name to me. If that is how I felt concerning my earthly father, how much more serious is it with my heavenly Father? He sacrificed the life of His Son to say to the world that sin is serious with God. It cost Him His Son to address the sin of the world. For me to sin without reference to Him would be a major blow to my relationship with God. He does not take that lightly. Every time I carry His name and live in a sinful way, I cause scores of others to misunderstand the holiness of God.

A pastor friend of mine was very active in helping others know how to live in Christ, but he began to commit adultery with a woman in his church. Another friend and I went to him immediately and with deep pleading we urged him to turn from his sin. He disregarded our counsel. He not only continued that relationship, but he divorced his wife, left the church where he was pastoring, created great tragedy in that congregation and enormous sorrow for his children, and finally married the woman. A few years later I was leading a conference where I was speaking on denying yourself, taking up your cross, and following Christ. He attended that conference. God used those messages to bring him under great conviction. He said, "I've got to talk with you." We went aside where he began to weep. He said, "Henry, this is the first time I've ever acknowledged this before anybody. I have deeply sinned against God. I have grievously dishonored my Lord. I have deeply sinned against my wife and my children and God's people. Would you pray for me?"

I said, "Oh, my brother, I will. But let me tell you how I'm going to pray for you. I'm going to pray that in your returning to God He will forgive you, but that He will deal with you in such a way that anybody who sees how God responds to you will be forever deterred from even thinking about committing this grievous sin." His face dropped. I turned to him and said, "I'm far more concerned about God's name than your name. I'm far more concerned about restoring God's reputation in the hearts of people than restoring your ministry. I care about you, but I want you to know I care far more about what you have done to God."

David understood sin from God's perspective and so his heart cry was with deep understanding. David cried out, "Blot out my transgressions!" Then he said, "Wash me thoroughly from my iniquity, and cleanse me from my sin" (Ps. 51:2).

Psalm 51:7–11 states:

> Purge me with hyssop, and I shall be clean;
> Wash me, and I shall be whiter than snow.
> Make me hear joy and gladness,
> That the bones You have broken may rejoice.
> Hide Your face from my sins,
> And blot out all my iniquities.
>
> Create in me a clean heart, O God,
> And renew a steadfast spirit within me.
> Do not cast me away from Your presence,
> And do not take Your Holy Spirit from me.

That is how to repent of your sin! Do you see your sin from God's perspective? David did. David cried to God from the depths of his soul, *Oh God, my sin—from Your perspective—is so grievous, I'm going to cry out to You with every ounce of my being until I know that You have dealt with me thoroughly and completely.* Notice he said, "*Then* I will teach transgressors Your ways, and sinners shall be converted to You" (Ps. 51:13). When I get my life right with

God, my life becomes a highway over which God can go to convince and convict others of their sin.

Then David said, "For You do not desire sacrifice, or else I would give it; You do not delight in burnt offering. The sacrifices of God are a broken spirit, a broken and a contrite heart—these, O God, You will not despise" (Ps. 51:16–17). David's spirit was utterly shattered when he saw his sin from God's perspective.

But he did two other things. In Psalm 51:3–4 David said, "For I acknowledge my transgressions, and my sin is always before me. Against You, You only, have I sinned, and done this evil in Your sight." Where did David do his sin, according to this Scripture? In God's sight. With God watching him. David knew God was watching, and he deliberately sinned anyway. David acknowledged he knew it. He did not make any excuse; he did not offer any rationalization. He simply said, "With You watching, I transgressed the clear guidance You have given me, and, oh, God, it was against You and You only that I have sinned. You are always just when You speak, and blameless when You judge. Oh, God, anything that

You do to deal with my sin is totally just. You are absolutely right. You have the right to do anything You want because sin is that serious with You."

Remember what God did. He did two major things. First, God said, "Now therefore, the sword shall never depart from your house, because you have despised Me, and have taken the wife of Uriah the Hittite to be your wife" (2 Sam. 12:10). All through the gospels, Jesus taught, "With the same *measure* you use, it will be *measured* to you" (Mark 4:24, emphasis added). That is the New Testament perspective. I express God's words this way: "David, you, by the sword of the Ammonites, took Uriah's life. Now I will not let a sword depart out of your home. David, your entire family is going to experience a sword in their lives because of your sin. Second, David, though I will not slay you, I will slay the child that is born because of your sin." How serious is sin from God's perspective?

When we look at our sin, we tend to cover it up. We say, *It is not all that bad. God is a loving God. He won't deal with me severely.* If you look at the Scripture from God's point of view, then you will cry unto God the way David did. Psalm 51 gave us David's perspective; now I want you to look at this same sin from God's perspective.

SIN FROM GOD'S PERSPECTIVE

God's view of David's sin is described in 2 Samuel 12. In this chapter you will see and understand why David cried out to God so deeply. Here we see sin from God's perspective. Remember, a whole year had probably passed and David had not dealt with his sin.

I have a feeling David was just like you and me. David did not experience any immediate consequences, so he assumed everything was okay. If we do not see the immediate consequences of our sin, we feel everything is fine with God. If God does not come and deal with us severely when we know we have sinned, we will probably assume it must be all right because there have not been any consequences. But you do not have to wait for the consequences—you can know from the Word of God whether what you did was sinful or not, and deal with it immediately. Do not let the sun go down on sin in your life (Eph. 4:26). Do not presume on the mercy and the grace of God. Deal with sin immediately.

In many ways we have an advantage over David, although he had the same Holy Spirit. God has given us in this present day the Holy Spirit whose assignment is to make sure that we are convicted when we sin. The gift of the Spirit of God is to help God's people know when they have sinned. He will bring to our remembrance the Scriptures, and He will remind us of God's standard. God will convince us of our sin and will plead with us to restore our relationship with Him.

I want you to see why David came to such a heart cry. Nathan told David the story of a poor man who owned nothing except one beautiful little ewe lamb. A rich man who had many sheep took the poor man's lamb and fed it to his house guest for dinner. David responded, *That man deserves to die.*

"Then Nathan said to David, 'You are the man!'" (2 Sam. 12:7).

What God said next is absolutely crucial, because it is much more serious for us than it was for David. God was putting David's sin in the context of the grace of God. The more God has done for us, the worse our sin is.

What was David before God made him king? He was a shepherd. What distance did God take David from being a shepherd to making him king over all of Israel? God had never been so good to anybody on the face of the earth as He was to David. So, before He let him see the seriousness of his sin, He reminded David of the context of his sin. Here is my paraphrase of verses eight and nine:

David, I anointed you king over Israel, and I delivered you from the hand of Saul. David, you did not escape because you were smarter or more skilled than Saul. I personally intervened, and I protected you. I gave you your master's house into your keeping. And I gave you the house of Israel and Judah. And if that had been too little, I would have given you much more. David, there is nothing that I have withheld from you. You sinned against the background of all My goodness to you. David, that makes your sin far worse than anyone else's, because I have never done as much for anyone else as I have done for you. David, when you sinned, you did it with the full knowledge of all I had done for you.

(2 SAM. 12:8–9)

Then Nathan said of David's sin, "Why have you despised the commandment of the LORD, to do evil in His sight?" (2 Sam. 12:9). God was saying, "David, for you to have blatantly committed this sin, you had to despise all of My teachings."

You may say concerning your sin, "Oh, God, I did not despise Your teachings, I just fell in a moment of weakness." That is your perspective. But look at it from God's perspective. God says for a Christian to sin willingly he has to do it against all the Spirit of God has been doing to teach him the ways of God. God gave us the Holy Spirit to be our teacher—to guide us into all truth—to teach us everything we need for a godly life. We have the Scripture in scores of translations. We have no excuse for our sin. We have all the grace of God.

God placed me in a godly family. Both of my grandmothers were godly women who prayed for me. God gave me a mother and father who walked with God with all of their hearts. They were pacesetters for my life, and they protected me and led me to know the Lord. My uncle, who baptized me, was in the great Shantung Revival as a missionary. A number of my relatives graduated from Spurgeon's College in London. They started Baptist churches all over England. I have a wonderful godly heritage. Do you understand that when I sin, I do so against the backdrop of the goodness of God? The effects would be enormous. You need to pray that God will keep my heart true to Him. He has allowed me to hold many public positions—if I were to sin, can you imagine the tragedy that would happen to those who know my life? Pray for me, that I will remain true to the Lord.

I have been trembling before the Lord as I read this,

because God saw David's sin against the backdrop of God's grace. But you and I have much more than David had, because we know what happened at the cross of Jesus Christ. We understand that the Son of God, though He was rich, became poor, that we, through His poverty, could be made rich (2 Cor. 8:9). We know "God so loved the world [and us] that He gave His only begotten Son" (John 3:16). We know far more than David did. We understand it cost God the Father the life of His Son to provide us with freedom from sin. We also know that God raised Him up and Jesus is interceding at the right hand of the Father for us. Do you realize there is not one of us who sins who does not do so against the advocacy of the Lord Jesus who is constantly at the right hand of the Father interceding for us? We sin against a lot more of the grace of God than David ever knew. Is that serious with God?

> We sin against a lot more of the grace of God than David ever knew. Is that serious with God?

You need to see something else from this passage in 2 Samuel 12:10. He said, "Now therefore, the sword shall never depart from your house, because you have despised Me." God said that for a child of His to deliberately sin, he has to despise God to do it. Now you may reason, *That is not how I look on it.* It does not matter how you look on it. It matters how God sees it! Revival will never come to the people of God until we view the awfulness of our sin as God does. Sin is never a light matter with God.

For David to sin, he had to despise the commandments of God—the teachings of the Lord. And we add to David's knowledge all that we know from the Gospels and all that we know from the entire New Testament. We have to despise the whole New Testament to continue in our sin. God said, "You have despised Me, David" (2 Sam. 12:10). But there is even a more tender moment that has gripped my heart as I see it from God's perspective.

Read on to verse 12 and following: "For you did it secretly, but I will do this thing before all Israel, before the sun." It is much more serious for leaders to sin than for an average person, because they influence so many. When leaders sin, God may choose to publicly expose them, and proclaim their transgression from the housetops. "So, David said to Nathan, 'I have sinned against the LORD.' And Nathan said to David, 'The LORD also has put away your sin; you shall not die. However, because by this deed you have given great occasion to the enemies of the LORD to blaspheme, the child also who is born to you shall surely die. [David, your sin gave an occasion for all of My enemies to blaspheme My name]" (2 Sam. 12:13–14).

When I read that, I wept and wept, "Oh, God, I love You with all of my heart."

But God would say, "Then deal with your sin, because there are enemies of Mine who are just waiting to find some of My children who are going to sin. And when they see you sin, or a church sin, it is going to give them great occasion to blaspheme My name."

I replied, "Oh, Lord, I did not know it was that serious."

"I know you did not," He answered, "or you wouldn't keep on sinning the way you do."

If you do not make it right with your brother, you sin against God and cause the enemies of God to blaspheme His name.

Do not give occasion for the enemies of God to blaspheme Him by the way you behave. You have the guidelines to love your brother—to prefer him over yourself. Read Philippians 2:5: "Let this mind be in you which was also in Christ Jesus." Let your brother serve in a more prominent position. Let

> Do not give occasion for the enemies of God to blaspheme Him by the way you behave.

your sister be the chairman of the committee. You be a master servant. Do not give any occasion for the enemies of God to blaspheme the name of your Lord.

"Oh, God, do not let my life give occasion to Your enemies to blaspheme Your name." I have been weeping my heart out before God saying, "Oh, God, do not let an idle word come out of my lips that dishonors You. Do not let me have an unguarded moment where something comes out of my mouth bringing great offense, causing the enemies of God to say, 'Oh, we have got something now. What is his God like that will not help him to live a godly life?'" And I pray, "Oh, God, help me to always remember my sin as You see it; not as I see it, but as You see it."

Some of you may be thinking, But Henry, that is Old Testament thinking only.

There is a New Testament passage that tells you that a New Testament Christian's sin is far more grievous to God than David's was. Hebrews 10, beginning with verse 26, reveals the heart of God. Sin is failing to do what the Spirit of God tells us we must do. It is refusing to walk by faith when He is inviting us to trust Him so He can demonstrate His greatness to a watching world. It is rebelling against the commands of God by not even trying to know what they are. It is justifying our transgressions rather than being brokenhearted over them.

"For if we sin willfully after we have received the knowledge of the truth, there no longer remains a sacrifice for sins, but a certain fearful expectation of judgment, and fiery indignation which will devour the adversaries" (Hebrews 10:26–27). He was not talking about unbelievers; He was speaking about God's people. Jesus was saying, "If you're not going with Me, you're going against Me." If you are choosing to not join God in His work, then you are deliberately moving against Him.

"Anyone who has rejected Moses' law dies without mercy on the testimony of two or three witnesses. Of how much worse punishment, do you suppose, will he be thought worthy who has trampled the Son of God underfoot, counted the blood of the covenant by which he was sanctified a common thing, and insulted the Spirit of grace?" (Heb. 10:28–29). For those who are God's people, how much worse punishment do you suppose will they be thought worthy than someone who has never known the grace of God? Then the writer of Hebrews describes how God sees the sins of the New Testament Christian. It says to me that there are three ways God sees my sin. God would say, "Henry, for you to sin, you have to tread the

Son of God under your feet. You have to walk all over the Son of God to do it. Second, you're going to be treating as common the blood of the covenant that set you apart and sanctified you as a child of God. And third, you're going to insult the Spirit of grace."

This is not describing an indiscretion or a bad habit or a weakness. It is saying that your sin deeply offends a holy God and invites His righteous wrath upon your life.

"For we know Him who said, "Vengeance is Mine, I will repay,' says the Lord. And again, "The LORD will judge His people" (Heb. 10:30). It is far more serious for Christians to sin than for unbelievers to do so, because for believers to sin, they do it against the knowledge of the truth and in spite of the wonderful acts of love and grace that have been freely bestowed upon them. For us to continue in our sin means that we treat Christ's death on the cross in vain, and we treat as worthless the blood Christ spilt on our behalf. We also quench the Spirit of grace, who has been convicting us of our sin.

The writer of Hebrews concludes by saying, "It is a fearful thing to fall into the hands of the living God" (Heb. 10:31). God is talking about us. Do you see your sin from God's perspective? Revival waits on the people of God to say,

Oh, God, forgive me. Oh, God, what have I done to You—what have I done to Your Son? How could I behave that way knowing it was sin, knowing it was contrary to Your will, knowing I was not walking by faith and causing others to not walk by faith—how could I possibly have done this in light of all that You have shown me? I would have had to reject all of Your grace to do that. How could I have told my church, "We cannot afford to do what God is telling us," and discouraged the hearts of God's people from taking a step of faith—how could I have done that after all we have experienced of Your grace? In so doing, I caused others to stumble.

It is inevitable that people will experience offenses, but probably the most severe statement Jesus made, in my opinion, is, "Whoever causes one of these little ones who believe in Me to sin, it would be better for him if a millstone were hung around his neck, and he were drowned in the depth of the sea. Woe to the world because of offenses! For offenses must come, but woe to that man by whom the offense comes!" (Matt. 18:6–7).

Do you know that if you speak up in a church business meeting and some young believers are there, and you leave the impression that God is unable to help your church do His will, and you confuse and discourage some of the believers from trusting God, "It is better," God said, "for you to have a millstone hung on your neck and be dropped into the deepest part of the sea." I shudder to think of how so many adults will one day have to give an account for how their actions turned the younger generation away from the Lord! He continued, "If your hand or foot causes you to sin, cut it off and cast it from you. It is better for you to enter into life lame or maimed, rather than having two hands or two feet, to be cast into the everlasting fire. And if your eye causes you to sin, pluck it out and cast it from you. It is better for you to enter into life with one eye, rather than having two eyes, to be cast into hell fire" (Matt. 18:8–9). I am not saying you will lose your eternal salvation. I am just quoting what Jesus said.

How serious is it? Second Chronicles 7:14 is still true: "If My people who are called by My name will humble themselves, and pray and seek My face, and turn from their wicked ways, then I will hear from heaven, and will forgive their sin and heal their land."

God's people must say, "Oh, God, it is me. God, I have sinned." They must pray and seek His face and cry out as David did and immediately turn from their wicked ways.

Dear people of God, please listen. God wants to see His people acknowledging that their sin is as serious as He says it is. He wants to hear that we are determined that sin will not reign in us. God wants to see us on our knees crying out to Him:

Oh, God, forgive me. I've not been the parent I should have been to my children. I know what I'm supposed to be, but I've quenched Your Holy Spirit when You told me to guide my children. Oh, God, You told me that I should pray and heaven would hear me, but I've not prayed. Oh, God, You told me to go out and share the Gospel with those who do not know You, but I have not done so. Oh, God, You told me to seek Your ways, and I've not sought them. Oh, God, I have sinned against You. But, oh, God, if You would have mercy on me and withhold from me what I rightly deserve, then I will immediately turn from my wicked ways and serve You with all of my heart.

The Scripture says that if we will respond this way, God will hear from heaven and forgive our sin. And then, do you know what will happen next? The great healing of America will begin to take place. When God's people return, then God's presence filling His people will be so powerful that multitudes will come under the conviction of their sin. People will see God's people taking their sin seriously. Then they will say, "If judgment is beginning at the house of God, what chance do we have?"

The great awakening in Wales saw one hundred thousand people joined to the churches in six months and countless people impacted around the world. Yet you rarely heard a sermon preached to unbelievers. Most of the sermons were preached to God's people. However, when the world saw God's people realizing how serious sin was in their lives, it brought them under severe conviction of their own sin. Atheists and agnostics watching God's people confess their sin and getting their lives right with God cried out, "Oh, me too! If those Christians need God and hate their sin, how much more do I need God to forgive me?" There is written testimony of agnostics coming to know Christ in the middle of a meeting of believers. As God's people began to weep over their sin, the former agnostics cried out to God, "Oh, God, have mercy on me! Blot out my

> The Scripture says that if we will respond, then God will hear from heaven and forgive our sin. And then, the great healing of America will begin to take place.

transgressions. Wash me thoroughly. Cleanse me. Deal with me. Create in me a clean heart, O God, and renew a steadfast spirit within me."

If we would cry out to God, there is no question that He would fill our lives with His mighty presence. Once God had us where He wanted us, He would immediately begin working through us to draw others to God. But the greatest single concern I have is what we have done to God's name. I repent not for what my sin has done to my life, but what it has done to Him. "Oh, God, how could I have done this to Your Son? How could I have done this to Your Holy Spirit? How could I have done this to You who, through the blood of Your Son, made a covenant with me that I would be set apart to be Yours? How could I have done this to You? Oh, God, have mercy."

Chapter 3

A HIGHWAY OF HOLINESS

A highway shall be there, and a road,
And it shall be called the Highway of Holiness.
The unclean shall not pass over it,
But it shall be for others.
Whoever walks the road, although a fool,
Shall not go astray.
No lion shall be there,
Nor shall any ravenous beast go up on it;
It shall not be found there.
But the redeemed shall walk there,
And the ransomed of the Lord shall return,
And come to Zion with singing,
With everlasting joy on their heads.
They shall obtain joy and gladness,
And sorrow and sighing shall flee away.

ISAIAH 35:8–10

THIS WAS AN AWESOME MOMENT WHEN GOD SPOKE TO Isaiah. Isaiah foresaw a time when God would establish a highway and it would be called *the highway of holiness*. God has not changed His agenda. Holiness is a highway for God. God has helped me to understand something of what that means. I have watched the Lord deal with my own life. I have also watched the Lord create a highway over which He is passing.

REVIVAL IN BROWNWOOD

Several years ago I was in Brownwood, Texas, with pastor John Avant. We spent four amazing days in which we led people into the presence of God. The awesomeness of God was so evident that people were profoundly impacted by God's holiness. People who were present spontaneously began to confess all manner of sin—in settings that were uncomfortable for them. The next morning when John arrived at his office, one of his laymen stood at his door weeping and said, "Pastor, I've got to repent." There were huge dimensions of his life that had been radically exposed as God worked in his life. On Sunday night, churches from twenty different denominations spontaneously closed their services and came to the church where God was moving. If you were to ask them, they would not have been able to tell you why they came. The presence of God had drawn them. When the invitation was extended, people responded with great weeping and utter brokenness before the Lord. Although people came from different denominations, it seemed as if they were one people with a terrible sense of what it means to stand in the presence of a holy God. In God's presence, all sin is exposed.

Could I dare say to you that wherever else you are, you are not in the presence of God if sin is not being exposed? You may simply be practicing religion if sin is not dealt with. You will know when you stand in the presence of a holy God. When God brings His word to bear upon people, it is profoundly different from when the Pharisees shared the Scriptures. When the Spirit of God takes the Word as a mighty sword, the Spirit of God pierces down to the soul, spirit, bone, and marrow. God's Word is a "discerner of the thoughts and intents of the heart" and it openly exposes the heart to a holy God (Heb. 4:12). You will know when the Spirit of God is wielding the Word of God.

God has held my life accountable to that truth. I must make sure that I am accountable to God. I might need to survey my own heart by saying, *Henry, don't keep saying that the Spirit of God is wielding the Word of God in you if sin can stay rampant in the life of everybody who hears God's Word from you. Don't keep fooling yourself. Your life is not a highway over which God is going. Your life is not a highway of holiness except when the Word of God in the hand of the servant of God acts like a sword.* If there is no exposure of sin when we speak, there is something wrong with the holiness of our lives. The Scripture says that when God builds a highway, it is a highway of holiness!

It had been an awesome four days as I spent time before the Lord with the people in Brownwood. I opened the Word of God and then watched it begin to move in ways I had never seen before. I had a deep burden for college students. We were on the campus of Howard Payne University for three days and nights. Tuesday night, when I finished presenting the Word of God, John and I watched to see not what we could do for God, but what God was doing in the midst of His people. John prayed, "Lord, if there's anybody that You have touched deeply that may need to share, would You bring him or her to me? I will not seek it out nor will I manipulate it."

Two young men came on their own initiative. They were broken. They had been in a time of prayer. For several weeks spontaneous prayer groups had broken out all over the campus. You could walk on that campus almost anywhere and see somebody praying. All across the dormitories, without any announcement, there were prayer groups. Some of them went through the night into the early morning. I must have had twenty students talk to me about a different prayer group that was meeting and ask if I wanted to join them. Some were in the tower, one was in a basement, one was in a dorm room, and some were in the chapel. There was a spontaneous sense that God in His holy presence had summoned them to pray.

Tuesday night when we had finished speaking, we asked those two young men if they would share. Both were respected leaders on the campus. One began in grave brokenness. He publicly admitted that he had been in bondage to pornography and lust. You could almost hear a gasp from the audience because these young men had been looked up to as leaders. They began to pour out their hearts explaining how they had been impure in their lives, and how it had shut down their prayer lives, and how they had an outward form of godliness—but all the power was gone. They had no power when they prayed and no power when they opened the Word of God.

Before the assembled group, these two young men began to pour out their hearts for God to have mercy on them, cleanse them, and make them pure and holy. With tears and brokenness, they began to talk about a deep desire for holiness in their lives. I turned and simply said, "Then if God has laid that on your heart and you have openly acknowledged that you have deeply sinned against God, would you go over there and pray? Are there others of you young men who have allowed pornography and lust and sin to grip your life and your heart? Would you come and pray?" It was like a steady stream, and then an avalanche. Students from all over that great auditorium began to come, and they filled the whole platform area—weeping, sobbing, and crying out to God.

Later, one after another, began to relate the horrific sin that had gripped their hearts. They would begin by saying, "I have been a Christian since I was young. I've grown up in the church," or, "I'm a pastor's child," or, "I'm a missionary's child," and then they would pour out their anguished hearts. Many of the young men turned to the young women and said, "Though I've not actually had sex with anybody, I just want you to know that

I have defiled you with my mind and my actions." A number of them said, "You girls, I ask you to forgive me. I just want you to know that I am so sorry for what I have been and what I have done." And they would just collapse on the platform in brokenness. The confession was agonizing.

Then a female student came and said, "You're saying it's just the men. Well, we women also have lust in our hearts." As she was describing with brokenness the sin in her heart, she said, "I ask you fellows to forgive me for the way I've dressed. I have not dressed like a Christian should. I ask you men to please forgive me. My heart and my mind and my life have been so full of sin."

I said to her, "I want you to go over to the piano and pray. Are there any others of you young women who are tired of your sin and who want to come and ask God to sweep across your mind and your heart and your life and make you clean? Would you come?"

The pastor told me later that it sounded like a stampede.

Those girls ran to the platform, and they began to sob even before they got there. They embraced one another and wept.

Older adults were there too. I said to the adults, "Are there some of you who need to come and pray also?" One of the men who came was a pastor. His son was a student at the university.

He looked over and said, "Son, I have been a role model before you, but before God and each of you, you need to know that I, too, have had lust and pornography in my mind and in my heart as a pastor." He said, "Son, forgive your dad. I've not been able to be the spiritual leader that God intended me to be." There was deep brokenness as God dealt with him.

I said, "Sir, you need to come down here. There may be other adults that need to come."

I thought to myself as I was listening and weeping along with them: The highway of holiness is something God creates, but when God creates a highway of holiness He exposes sin like a refiner's fire.

Three-and-a-half hours later I said, "There may be some who need to leave."

The pastor later told me, "Henry, there were people on their faces before God all night long. They never went to bed."

Tuesday we had a noon luncheon, and it was full. There were maybe twenty or twenty-five different denominational groups, business people, and key leaders present. We were just about to close our time together when the dear pastor wisely said, "Now before we bring our bene-diction, is there anyone who would like to speak to God in confession of your sin?"

Some pastors in that group began to cry out, "Oh, God, my mind is so full of filth! My heart is so full of sin and lust!" We were standing, waiting to finish, and people all over began to acknowledge that they had sinned griev-ously against God.

I lingered a long time talking with people afterward. An elderly lady with two canes feebly made her way up to me. When she looked at me, tears streamed down her face. She said, "I'm eighty-eight years old, and I desire purity before God more than anything in all the world. Do you think God could make me clean and use me at eighty-eight?"

I said, "Young lady, God's about to give you the best days of your life. God is creating a highway of holi-ness for you."

"Oh," she said, "I desire holiness more than anything in the world!"

What I see happening is that God is creating *a highway of holiness*. And I say with all the reverence of

What I see happening is that God is creating *a highway of holiness*. And I say with all the reverence of my soul—*the unclean will not walk on it!* They will not!

69

my soul—*the unclean will not walk on it!* They will not! It is for others. It is for those who understand the awesome holiness of God! I believe we have a generation that has no experience of or reference point for revival. We also have a generation that has almost no reference point for a genuine experience of the holiness of God. You cannot talk about the holiness of God without, at the same time, the refiner's fire touching every corner of your life, leaving it completely exposed before Him. When you read the Word of God, it's like a hammer. It's like a fiery blaze. You cannot turn anywhere without everything in your heart and life being exposed to God. Holy God does not play games. If you have a heart that is hardened, or if you have filled your mind with video games and television, you can enter the presence of God and be oblivious to what He is doing. Your heart and mind are too cluttered to hear what God is saying.

FAITHFUL TO GOD'S WORD

I was in Nairobi ministering to a large group of missionaries from all over that continent shortly after the Rwandan genocide. As best as I knew how, I sought to minister to those anguished missionaries with the Word of God. Everyone who hears you speak knows whether you have come from the presence of God. God won't allow His people to fail to recognize whether they are merely hearing a sermon or if it is a word from God. God is very serious. There is a sense that God is heightening the hunger and thirst in the hearts of His people. Before you speak on God's behalf, you need to have that Word washed over your own heart and life first.

All of this was going through my heart and mind as I was about to speak to the missionaries from Rwanda. They had seen such horrible things. They had cried unto God. Many native pastors, their dear wives, and their children had been butchered. I knew that the missionaries came from South Africa to Ethiopia to that meeting. Some had been imprisoned, some had friends who had been killed, and some had been harmed by the conflict. One of the missionary wives who came had soldiers break into her house. They had beaten up her husband and then raped her repeatedly while her little children were in the back of the house. Now she was being tested for AIDS.

I do not know about you, but when I am speaking to a group of frontline warriors, I tremble! I said, "Oh, God, when I open this book, I tremble. These dear people need to see the blazing holiness of God, because they are filled with what sin can do. They are immersed in what evil can do, but, oh, God, somehow they need to stand in Your holy presence and experience what only You can do." So, I took the Bible and began to share. It was one of those rare and wonderful moments. I believe there will be no revival without holiness in the leadership. None. Cry unto God all you want. He will not hear you. Pull together all the phrases that revivalists of previous generations have used, and it will not make an ounce of difference to the heart of God. God is looking for holiness!

While I was sharing with those dear missionaries, I said, "Who am I to be here?" That was one of those times I wished there was another one who was speaking so I could listen and cry with them. But I was the one assigned to speak. I was opening the Word of God, taking the verses, and saying, "See *this* God, see this? That's your God. That's Him. He's with you." Suddenly one of the men jumped up and began to weep right in the middle of my sharing. He said, "Oh, God, I need holiness in my life." I hadn't even talked about holiness. I hadn't even mentioned it. But I did bring him through the Word of God into the presence of a holy God.

Suddenly others began to get up, and say, "Oh, I need holiness in my life too."

Then one of the missionaries declared, "I'm going to go home and trash every video that we have in our home. Since we don't get TV, we purchased videos, and we were not careful in what we bought. There's so much filth and ungodliness we've allowed our children to see. My wife and I said, 'It's just got a little blasphemy in it, but it has a good story line.'"

That is like saying *No, Lord!* There is no such thing as a little blasphemy that has a good story line. Those cancel each other out. You just removed the good story when you filled it with blasphemy. I have heard a lot of pastors say, "Well, it has good moral lesson in it, a little blasphemy here, some mild pornography there." If you put that in your heart, I guarantee you, God will not hear you when you pray. He absolutely will not. An impure mind and heart do not even know how to pray.

> There is no such thing as a little blasphemy that has a good story line. Those cancel each other out.

I have found that I cannot pray when there is sin in my life. Oh, I can say some pious sounding words, but I just want to hang my head in shame and say, *Oh, God, You knew that everything I said was to cover the sin that I have not been willing to deal with in my life. I just let it run across my life, and I've excused it.* But the Lord does not let you do that. Throughout my time with those missionaries, there was a spontaneous awareness of the holiness of God, and a return to a godly and pure life.

When their hearts were right, many of the men instantly realized that they were mistreating their wives— those precious gifts from God, chosen for them from before the world.

I told my wife, "Marilyn, when I knelt at the altar to marry you, I was scared half to death."

"Oh," she said, "I wasn't. I was having a good time."

I said, "That bothered me. You were having such a wonderful time."

She said, "Well, why did you feel so scared?"

"Oh," I said. "Let me tell you why. Do you know when God had a purpose for your life? Before the world was made! For twenty-one years, holy God was shaping your life. He put Scriptures into your heart as a little girl. He caused you to feel the call of missions when you were a young girl involved in a missions education program. He took you to college and He shaped your life for Himself, and then He took that tender, precious, clean life and He gave it to me. When I was at the altar, I said, *Oh, God, help me to care for her as Your servant.*" And then I said, "Marilyn, tell me every commitment you have ever made

74

to God. I'll spend the rest of my life helping you fulfill those commitments." I have held her life as a sacred trust.

When those missionaries came into the presence of a holy God and faced Him, God began to wash them with the Scriptures. He specifically and deeply turned their minds, hearts, wills, and souls against what had been offensive to Him. The men looked around and the moment they saw their dear wives, they wept their hearts out. They knew they had not treated them as they should. Suddenly they were looking at their wives as a sacred trust they had mishandled, and they wept.

With increasing intensity I have seen that of absolute necessity, the highway over which revival comes, is the *highway of holiness*. Since God is holy, our lives must also be holy.

REVIVAL PRAYING

I have been in many meetings that had a focus on revival. My own heart has had a sensitivity toward revival since I was a teenager. God placed a burden on my heart for revival for my nation at a very young age.

Psalm 24 needs to be applied when praying for revival:

Who may ascend into the hill of the LORD?
Or who may stand in His holy place?
He who has clean hands and a pure heart,
Who has not lifted up his soul to an idol,
Nor sworn deceitfully.
He shall receive blessing from the LORD,
And righteousness from the God of his salvation.
This is Jacob, the generation of those who seek Him,
Who seek Your face. Selah

Lift up your heads, O you gates!
And be lifted up, you everlasting doors!
And the King of glory shall come in.
Who is this King of glory?
The LORD strong and mighty,
The LORD mighty in battle.
Lift up your heads, O you gates!
Lift up, you everlasting doors!
And the King of glory shall come in.
Who is this King of glory?
The LORD of hosts,
He is the King of glory. Selah

PSALM 24:3–10

Who can ascend the hill of the Lord? And who can stand in His holy place? "He who has clean hands and a pure heart, who has not lifted up his soul to an idol, nor sworn deceitfully. He shall receive blessing from the LORD, and righteousness from the God of his salvation" (vv. 4–5).

I am deeply convinced that praying for revival is an offense to God if we do not have a clean heart. It is almost blasphemy to dare to come into the presence of a holy God and ask Him to bless us when our hearts are not clean before Him. Praying for revival has a prerequisite. Who can ascend the hill of the Lord? Who can stand in His holy place? Who can stand in His presence? Who can stand in the throne room—*the most holy place*—as Hebrews 10 describes it?

One of the great deterrents to revival and awakening is that we do not hold ourselves accountable. We read the Word of God but do not hold ourselves accountable to see it implemented in our lives. This Scripture says that if we meet the conditions of holiness in our lives, He will bless us.

Are you looking to see if there is an obvious touch of God on your life and ministry? Do you minister week after week—yet none of God's people comes under conviction? Do you talk to the leaders in your church knowing they are full of sin and yet they have absolutely no sense of the holiness of God? How can a holy man stand in their presence and yet they not feel God's presence? The Scripture says that when our lives are what God wants them to be, His blessing upon us will be obvious.

There have been times I have wept and wept before the Lord and said, Lord, I'm a sinner at best, and You're going to have to work powerfully in my life until I'm where You want me to be. I'll know I'm in a right relationship with You when You begin to work through my life to implement your word, obviously and openly, in the hearts of the people I relate to.

But we do not hold ourselves accountable. We do not say, I'm going to look to see if God is doing anything through my life. If nothing is happening, I will be deeply grieved in my heart. I will not be able to stand it if God has not done a work through me to minister to His people.

I talk with many pastors who describe their churches as being rebellious and disoriented to God. A question I ask them is, "How long have you been there?"

Many reply, "I've been there five—or even seven, ten, or fifteen—years."

I reply, "Then the people in the church are the product of your walk with God. You ought not to have been with

78

a people for five years or more and the holiness of God to not absolutely come over the people. The holiness of God should be so real in your own life that when you speak, there is a sense of holy awe that you have obviously been in the presence of almighty God."

We sometimes say we have been in the presence of God, but everything God says will happen when we are in His presence is absent—and we do not hold ourselves accountable. I feel that it is time for us to say, *It's me, oh, Lord*. If there is nothing happening that God says will occur when His servant is where God wants him to be, then it ought to grieve our heart. We ought to have a brokenness of spirit that says, *Oh, God, I will not rest. I cannot rest at night unless I know that this servant is what You want him to be. I'll know that I am when I walk among Your people and they encounter You in such a profound way that it cannot be explained except that they came face to face with the awesome presence of almighty God in my life.*

Do you hold yourself accountable as a servant of God? Do you look at the Scriptures and say, *If God says this, then this is what will happen when a person walks with God?* There is a profound accountability when you tell your people that you walk with God. Your people should expect to see in your life everything Scripture claims should be evident in a servant of God who walks with Him. Please do not excuse the fact that none of this is happening in your life and then tell the people, *But God has called me!* It is an affront to holy God and to His dear people to claim that you have a word from God when you do not. If you do not have a word from God, you should refrain from speaking.

> There is an incredible hunger in the hearts of God's people.

There is an incredible hunger in the hearts of God's people. It is amazing what happens when a person who walks with God, opens the Word of God. I have found that people respond very positively to messages on repentance. Over the last few years when I have spoken on repentance, I have seen altars filled with God's people dealing with their sin. I have watched pastors, laypeople, youth, and college students come to repent by the score. I have watched them come in absolute brokenness before the Lord. It may be hard to believe, but I have not had one word of criticism from the people of God to whom I spoke concerning repentance. They say, *We've been waiting for someone to tell us what to do. Our hearts are so full of sin, and we didn't know how to break its bondage.*

If I could have gathered up all the brokenness and sin

those college students at Howard Payne confessed, it would have been a mountain. I shared with the faculty by saying, "Some of you professors, if these same children—these same young people—can be in your classes week after week and still carry that utter brokenness of sin, there's something wrong with your teaching. These students are right now weeping their hearts out saying, 'I would have given anything if someone had helped me get rid of this awful sin years ago. I've got such brokenness in my life, and it is accumulating, and no one spoke about it.'" I then turned to the pastors and said, "Do you recognize any of these students? Do you know they have been sitting in your churches week after week?" There's something wrong with our preaching and our worship if the young people coming to our churches can be filled so full of sin and yet be unaffected by our worship services each week.

As pastors we should each grieve before the Lord and say, Oh, Lord, if Your people can be immersed in sin and listen to me preach week after week without any change, then there's something wrong with this preacher. Not with them, but with me. What is it that's missing in my life? What is it in my ministry that God is not honoring? What is it that God refuses to do until I make radical changes in my life?

HOLINESS AND THE JUDGMENT OF GOD

Psalm 24 fits well in the midst of a passage in James. Psalm 24:3 says, "Who may stand in His holy place?" Then in James 5, this truth is given: *The effective, fervent prayer of a righteous man avails much."* Is that not true? Do you know what I believe to be one of our greatest dangers? We have all the truth in our heads, but it has never touched our hearts. Do you know how you can tell if the truth has touched your heart? According to Jesus it is spiritually impossible to have your heart in one condition and the fruit of your life in another. If we claim to believe God's truth from His Word, and we assume those truths are in our hearts, yet we see no evidence of those truths in our lives, then the Scripture is in our heads but it has never made it into our hearts.

You will know the truth has gone from your head to your heart when the change in your life is obvious to you and to those around you. You will know if the truth has reached your heart if it is bearing fruit in your life. When it bears fruit in your life, it will begin to bear fruit in a world around you as well.

We have conditioned ourselves to fill our heads with truth. We think that because we attend several Bible studies each week and we believe a biblical theology, that the truth of Scripture is implemented in our lives.

If you were to talk to many pastors and say, "Do you believe in prayer?" many would say, "Absolutely."

Then you could ask, "Do you pray?"

They might answer, "Well, that's been the weak point of my life and ministry."

I would say, "Your problem is that you do not believe in prayer. You do not believe in the God who issues a summons to come before Him. If the love of God and prayer were truly in your heart, you would pray. You have the truth in your head, but it has never reached your heart."

Have you ever been summoned by God into His holy presence? Did you come into His presence when He invited you? Did you stay there until God transformed you with His Word? Has that Word so changed your heart that people wondered what in the world happened to you? That is when the truth that comes from the mouth of God has gone from your head to your heart. When it is assimilated into your heart, it impacts the way you live. Jesus taught that the fruit of people's lives indicates what is in their heart. We keep claiming that we believe the truth. We insist, *I believe in revival. I believe in awakening.* But do you remember the words of Joel? "'Now, therefore,' says the LORD,

'Turn to Me with all your heart, with fasting, with weeping, and with mourning.' So rend your heart, and not your garments; return to the LORD your God, for He is gracious and merciful, slow to anger, and of great kindness; and He relents from doing harm" (Joel 2:12–13). I don't know what you do with that Scripture, but let me tell you what I do. Did you hear God's command? What did He tell the Levites to do? *Wail. Mourn. Grieve.* That is a command. We have it in our heads, but it has never touched our hearts. You will know when it hits your heart. You will cry like Jeremiah did: "Oh, that my head were waters, and my eyes a fountain of tears, that I might weep day and night for the slain of the daughter of my people!" (Jer. 9:1).

We can read these verses and identify the book of Joel with America and yet never respond to the command of God. It is the spiritual leaders who must grieve. Now, when you read Joel 2:12–13, what do you do with it? It is a command and it is a condition for God's withholding His hand of judgment. Do you believe that if we will not follow that command, the judgment of God will come? I have said to myself, *Oh, Lord, what have I done when I've stood in Your holy presence? You are a holy God. The way of revival is the way of holiness. That means anytime You speak, I bring my life into Your presence and let You change it. You match my heart with Your heart.*

We have been using the correct terminology about revival but have not let it penetrate our hearts. When was the last time the pain over the spiritual condition of your nation was so heavy in your heart that you could not bear it? When was the pain so grievous that you could not find words to speak? I do not know about you. I just know what God is doing in my life. God is saying, *Henry, it's time for accountability. Don't you ever come to My Word and see what I say and not make certain it goes from your head, to your heart, to your life, to the rest of the world around you.* We must be willing to let God come as a refiner's fire—a launderer's soap—until He has refined us like silver and gold.

In James 5:17–18 the Scripture shares that Elijah was a man who had a nature just like yours and mine. But there was a difference—he prayed. Well, that is half the difference. What is the most important difference? When he prayed, God did something. Have you been praying for revival? Most of you would say, *Amen.* What evidence do you see that God has heard you? Are you not concerned about heaven's silence? Is America not desperate for revival? Has God put it on your heart to pray for revival? Have you ever held yourself accountable to the Scripture that says, "The prayer of a righteous man is powerful and effective" (James 5:16 NIV)? Elijah prayed and it did not rain. Elijah prayed again and God sent a deluge and the whole of Israel returned to God. If you understand that Scripture, does it bother you when you pray and yet nothing happens? I have gone before the Lord and said, *Lord, I've got to see Your answer to my prayers. Not for my sake, not for the people's sake, but for Your name's sake. Lord, it's not a matter of me just praying. It's a matter of after I pray, seeing you respond to my request.*

I went back to 1 Kings 18. This chapter should be a pattern for our praying as well.

> And it came to pass, at the time of the offering of the evening sacrifice, that Elijah the prophet came near and said, "Lord God of Abraham, Isaac, and Israel, let it be known this day [number 1] that You are God in Israel [number 2] and I am Your servant [number 3], and that I have done all these things at Your word. Hear me, O Lord, hear me, that this people may know that You are the Lord God, and that You have turned their hearts back to You again.

> 1 Kings 18:36–37

Do you hold yourself accountable when God lays that Scripture on your heart? Do you ask, *Oh, God, at which point in this process am I grossly deficient in my walk with*

You? Is it that I have never heard You say that there will be no rain? Is it that I am not close enough to You to hear or even know what You are saying? Is it that I have not had a word from You so You will not do anything when I pray? Where in this process have I fallen short of what you are looking for?

My heart says, *Oh, God, is there not a point in our lives where, if that passage in James is true, then we could follow that pattern and say, "Lord, would You make certain that I understand what it means to be a righteous man, to have holiness as the pattern of my life so I can stand on Your holy hill? You have dealt with me about sin in my life and the need for holiness to be a part of my life so that when I stand in Your holy place, I hear what You say. When I stand in Your holy place, my ears are open, my eyes are alert, and my heart is tender because I am free of sin. You have thoroughly dealt with my sin. My ears hear Your voice, my eyes understand what You are doing, and my heart responds immediately. I can go from that moment and declare that there is a word from the Lord and You will respond—that the people will know that You are God—and there is at least one servant who is serving You and listening to You and proclaiming Your word."*

How is God answering your prayers? Does God respond? This is the point at which we must be accountable to God. All through the Scriptures God says the *highway*

> You have thoroughly dealt with my sin. My ears hear Your voice, my eyes understand what You are doing, and my heart responds immediately.

over which He goes, the *highway* over which God's people travel, is the *way of holiness*. That is especially true when God puts prayer on our hearts. When God invites us to pray, and He has made us clean by His word, then He is pleased to act on our behalf. But if He does not respond, it is at that point that we should hold ourselves accountable. Now, could I put it this way? Did God's response to Elijah, bringing revival to His people, depend on all of the people getting their lives right with God? No, one person got his life right with God. Then the Scripture says in 1 Kings 18:37: "that this people may know that You are the LORD God, and that You have turned their hearts back to You again." It took one person, taking his walk with God seriously, for an entire nation to feel the impact.

All over the nation peoples' hearts are returning to God. God initiates that. But my heart cry is to say it is crucial that we hold ourselves accountable to a life of holiness. If we will walk righteously, God will answer our prayers. Our lives will be a *highway* over which God will come.

Remember how John the Baptist preached in Luke

3:4: "Prepare the way of the Lord; Make His paths straight. [Make a highway for our God.]" That highway is the *highway of holiness*. It is a clean and pure heart that sees God. Jesus said, "Blessed are the pure in heart, for they shall see God" (Matt. 5:8). It is that quality of walk that God uses as the *highway* over which He will move mightily in revival. I have been with so many people who have prayed for revival with their lips, but their hearts had not known the cleansing touch of holy God. I am not saying that to be critical. I know how my own heart was for so long. I know how easy it is for me to say the words and feel that as long as I express the proper pious phrases, that He will know I am serious. God says, *You'll know when you have met the conditions of holiness when you see Me move in mighty power through your life and through your church out to the ends of the earth.*

There is one other Scripture I want us to consider; then I want to give a practical approach to what is hindering holiness in our lives. Notice Hebrews 12 beginning in verse seven.

> If you endure chastening, God deals with you as with sons; for what son is there whom a father does not chasten? But if you are without chastening, of which all have become partakers, then you are illegitimate

and not sons. Furthermore, we have had human fathers
who corrected us, and we paid them respect. Shall we
not much more readily be in subjection to the Father
of spirits and live? For they indeed for a few days chastened us as seemed best to them, but He for our profit,
that we may be partakers of His holiness.

HEBREWS 12:7–10

When I disciplined my children, I did it in a way I felt
was best. But when God chastens, He has a goal in mind.
He says that He disciplines us for our profit that we may be
partakers of His holiness. "Now no chastening seems to be
joyful for the present, but painful; nevertheless, afterward
it yields the peaceable fruit of righteousness to those who
have been trained by it. Therefore strengthen the hands
which hang down, and the feeble knees" (Heb. 12:11–12).
I underlined *the feeble knees.* What does that symbolize?
Could it be our prayer life? We must strengthen our prayer
life deeply and then make straight paths for our feet so the
lame may not be turned aside but rather be healed. I held
my life up against this Scripture when I was at Howard
Payne University that weekend. I said, *Oh, God, would
You help me to deal with my walk with You in such a way
that those who are stumbling all over the place will not be*

turned aside and their knees weakened, but that they will be healed?

I do not know how you respond to a Scripture like that, but I said, *Oh, God, I earnestly ask You to deal with me so that the students on this campus will be healed and not hindered in their walk with You.* Then I looked to see if any of the students were being healed, because I did not want to go to the next assignment and say, *Oh, God, do the same thing. Now, You didn't do it for me the last four times but, Lord, I'm going to ask You to do it this time.* I said, *Oh, Lord, I'll know if You have helped me to become the kind of person You want me to be, if the chastening You are doing in my mind and heart is making me a partaker of Your holiness. I'll know you are working in me when those I am relating to are being healed, when those entrapped in pornography are radically set free, when those who are caught up in lust are delivered and experience Your joy once again.*

So many of those students wept and tried to describe the change that had taken place while they were on the platform. They had experienced the cleansing touch of the living Lord. Speak about a lame man dancing—that was what was happening! They didn't know how to describe it. One of the young men said, "I don't know, I'm just so happy. I'm just so free. I feel as though I've been healed!" I said, "My brother, you were healed."

Lord, would You discipline me as thoroughly as you must until I am a partaker of Your holiness so that when the spiritually lame are present and Your Word is shared, that a highway to God is present and they can make their way to God on it and be healed? If no one is being healed when you speak to them, the problem is not the Word of God or those who need to be healed. The problem is with you.

> The tragedy is that God has placed so many of us in places of leadership and yet so little healing is being done in the lives of His people.

The tragedy is that God has placed so many of us in places of leadership and yet so little healing is being done in the lives of His people. There seems to be no grief over that. There is no brokenness. We claim that it is just the way people are these days. We put the blame everywhere else. Revival comes through God-appointed leaders. God calls us as He did Elijah and says, "I will fashion you and shape you until you have a message to give and then I will enable you to deliver that word. Then I will hold you accountable to do what I say and people will know that

I am God and you are My servant and everything you've done has come from Me."

Let me ask you, when was the last time God clearly demonstrated His power through your life to the people where you serve? If you have to insist that they follow you, you are in trouble. If you have to claim your authority as the pastor of a church so people support you, you should be concerned. Do you know when they will follow you? When God puts it in their hearts to do so. When God can trust your leadership and when God has a servant like Elijah. This verse is enormous if you take it seriously. *Lord, help Your people to know that You turn people's hearts back to You.*

I think it is time that we quit blaming the people for not responding to our leadership. The Scripture says if God has a servant who walks in holiness, He will cause the people's hearts to turn to Him. Do you remember the last part of Malachi 4? He says He will turn the hearts of the fathers to their children. How would you know if God had done that for you? What did He say He would do? He said He would turn the hearts of the children to the fathers. Now I take this very simply: *Lord, I'll know when You have turned my heart to my children sufficiently when I see You turning the hearts of my children back to me. And I will not use that Scripture until I see that happening.*

Some of you have children who are a far from the Lord, and you have prayed for them. You must remain in God's presence until He turns your heart toward your children. It is a profound thing for God to turn the heart of a father to his children. This involves far more than merely giving them some extra attention or calling them every Saturday night. It does not mean God turns your head toward your children; He turns your heart toward your children. You will know when God has turned your heart fully to your children when you see God turning the hearts of your children back to you.

I have not heard many preach on this as one of the prerequisites for spiritual awakening. In Luke 1:17 God puts it this way: "He will also go before Him in the spirit and power of Elijah, 'to turn the hearts of the fathers to the children,' and the disobedient to the wisdom of the just, to make ready a people prepared for the Lord." I am convinced that one of the great prerequisites for revival is what He does with the men toward their families. He makes ready a people prepared for the Lord.

> Therefore strengthen the hands which hang down, and the feeble knees, and make straight paths for your feet, so that what is lame may not be dislocated, but rather be healed. Pursue peace with all people, and

holiness, without which no one will see the Lord: looking carefully lest anyone fall short of the grace of God;
lest any root of bitterness springing up cause trouble,
and by this many become defiled; lest there be any
fornicator or profane person like Esau, who for one
morsel of food sold his birthright.

HEBREWS 12:12–16

There are some spiritual leaders who for one careless
moment of sexual temptation have sold their spiritual
birthright. I am disturbed by the number of people who
try to get sexually immoral people, who claim they have
repented, back into the ministry. I am very hard on that.
Anyone who can commit sexual sin has a character flaw.
God will forgive your sin, but it takes time to transform
your character. As a result, we are allowing carnal people
back into our pulpits. The Word of God is clear. Many
who have been sexually immoral now want to come back
saying, *God forgave me,* yet there is absolutely *no* evidence
of repentance whatsoever. I am concerned about what
we are doing to these people and to the organizations
they lead.

Can you imagine applying that same thinking to
Esau? *Well, he repented. Well, he tried to get his birthright*

back. That is exactly right, but it was not given back to him. *He sought it with tears.* That is right, but he did not get it back. Holiness means that God is holy. We have plenty of evidence in the Scripture of the nature of that holiness. This Scripture says Esau sold his birthright for a morsel of food. You know that afterward, when he wanted to inherit the blessing, he was rejected for he found no place for repentance, though he sought it diligently with tears. That is because of the holiness of God.

The Scripture says we need to pursue holiness. That is, we need to let the full measure of the nature of God become the pattern for our characters. We need to let Him form in us the righteousness of Christ. We need to let Him take every part of our minds and our hearts and keep them holy unto Himself. If you keep allowing profanity and immorality into your mind so that when you try to pray, you cannot, then do not pray for revival, because He will not grant it. When you regularly draw near to God and stand in His awesome presence, the character and holiness of God will absolutely overwhelm you.

How does God's holiness impact your life? Do you find

How does God's holiness impact your life? Do you find yourself trembling when God speaks?

yourself trembling when God speaks? The other day I turned in the Word and when I read it, there came over my life a total trembling from top to bottom. I found myself spontaneously weeping. I was literally trembling. I said, *Oh God, suddenly You made me aware of how holy You are and how sinful I am and how much is at stake when I handle sacred things. When I read this book I am made aware of how much of eternity hangs in the balance and when I speak with people, how much You have in Your heart for them. Lord, I am totally unworthy of that awesome responsibility. Oh God, if this is true, then don't let me ever speak again in Your name. Your holiness and my sinfulness are so far apart.*

I lay there without any strength. I said, *Oh, God, how could I possibly speak?* He said, *I'll do in you what I did in Isaiah. He had no right to speak either, but I took some coals and put them on his lips. You'll know when I've done that for you.*

I said, *Then, Lord, hold me accountable for holiness. Lord, don't let me just talk about it. Don't let me just read about it. You said it was the highway of holiness that would bring the people back to You and they would rejoice and they would sing.*

Many of our church services sound like funerals. I

have watched some congregations sing praise songs, and if you looked at them five minutes later you would think you were in a funeral service. Singing about holiness is not the same thing as being holy! Praise songs are no substitute for a clean heart. We are leaving people in a terrible condition. We desperately need to have lives that walk in holiness with Him.

Holiness is the highway over which God brings revival. Without holiness, no one will see the Lord. No one can stand in His holy presence without clean hands and a pure heart. It is the pure in heart who see God. May the Spirit of God teach us when we pray, not to say, *Oh God, help me to see You,* without saying at the same time, *Oh God, give me the conditions of heart that are prerequisite to seeing You. I cannot ask You to make Yourself real to me unless I also ask You to do a cleansing work in my heart, mind, and will, because only then will I see You. To ask You to let me see You in all of Your glory without the prerequisite of clean hands is utter foolishness.* He will not do it.

> I wonder why we have cried to the Lord and seen so little.

I wonder why we have cried to the Lord and seen so little. Could it be that God is waiting for His servants to walk over the *highway of holiness* to God? The unclean will not walk on it. The clean—those the Lord has ransomed and redeemed from all of their sin, dressed in His righteousness, and who are now free in heart and mind before Him—will!

Ask God if a Scripture has been used by God to quicken your heart and conscience. We are talking about revival. We are speaking about the survival of our nation. We are considering the eternal destinies of millions. We are talking about the honor of our Lord. We are focusing on the glory of His name. We are talking about being His servants. We are seeing the people of God in great distress, yet with nothing changing in their lives even though they just attended a worship service.

Let us say, *Oh, Lord, begin this process in me. Do whatever You must do.* Do not take this lightly, but with a sober, clear understanding of His Word.

> "And the Lord, whom you seek,
> Will suddenly come to His temple,
> Even the Messenger of the covenant,
> In whom you delight.
> Behold, He is coming,"
> Says the LORD of hosts.

"But who can endure the day of His coming?
And who can stand when He appears?
For He is like a refiner's fire
And like launderers' soap.
He will sit as a refiner and a purifier of silver;
He will purify the sons of Levi,
And purge them as gold and silver,
That they may offer to the LORD
An offering in righteousness."

MALACHI 3:1–3

That is where we are. Revival waits on the holiness of God's people. May God grant you a quickened heart that you may seek holiness with every fiber of your being. If there is anything that the Spirit of God brings to your mind that must be dealt with, then would you—with all of your heart, for His sake, ask God to cleanse you?

Father, in the magnitude of Your grace You have permitted a number of us to be present when we saw what Your holiness can do. You took a group of profane children of Yours who knew they were in sin. But they had nothing that was bringing them to conviction. Suddenly, You began to work in Your people and their lives began to be cleansed and made whole. Their presence began, like leaven, to affect their families, fellow students, and colleagues across the campus. You touched some so deeply that they openly acknowledged the abominable nature of their sin, but they also stood to give witness to Your grace. Lord, the moment they did, Your holiness fell on a whole group of people. Lord, would You shape our lives as leaders until holiness is characteristic of us? We'll know that holiness is in place by what happens in the lives of those we encounter.

Oh, Father, these are most sacred, holy moments. We sense that heaven stands hushed. All the work of redemption is focused on our response to Your holiness. The highway that You have purposed waits on our consecration. You have given us a pattern to be holy as You are holy. Forgive us when we have explained our sin away. Father, in Your Word You have told us that leaders must be blameless. Oh, Lord, do not let us excuse that away. May we be blameless as we stand before Your people and before a watching world. Oh, God, may these days create a mighty highway for You, that out of the holiness of our lives, You may with mighty power demonstrate that we have become what You are looking for and that You have heard our cry, as we pray in our holiness, and that You have granted our requests. May we see the evidence in the lives of Your people who live their lives before a watching world. May your awesome, holy presence be clearly evident in and through our lives and ministry. Now we ask You to guide us through these moments of personal response to You and we ask it in Your name, Amen.

PRAYING THE SCRIPTURES

Selections to Draw You Closer to God

FOR COMFORT KNOWING GOD IS WITH YOU

And He said, "My Presence will go with you, and I will give you rest."

Exodus 33:14

"And the Lord, He is the One who goes before you. He will be with you, He will not leave you nor forsake you; do not fear nor be dismayed."

Deuteronomy 31:8

"Have I not commanded you? Be strong and of good courage; do not be afraid, nor be dismayed, for the Lord your God is with you wherever you go."

Joshua 1:9

"The LORD is near to those who have a broken heart,
And saves such as have a contrite spirit."

PSALM 34:18

"Surely He shall deliver you from the snare of the fowler
And from the perilous pestilence.
He shall cover you with His feathers,
And under His wings you shall take refuge;
His truth shall be your shield and buckler.
You shall not be afraid of the terror by night,
Nor of the arrow that flies by day."

PSALM 91:3–5

"Through the LORD's mercies we are not consumed,
Because His compassions fail not.
They are new every morning;
Great is Your faithfulness."

LAMENTATIONS 3:22–23

"Fear not, for I am with you;
Be not dismayed, for I am your God.
I will strengthen you,

Yes, I will help you,
I will uphold you with My righteous right hand."

ISAIAH 41:10

The Spirit Himself bears witness with our spirit that we are children of God.

ROMANS 8:16

For I am persuaded that neither death nor life, nor angels nor principalities nor powers, nor things present nor things to come, nor height nor depth, nor any other created thing, shall be able to separate us from the love of God which is in Christ Jesus our Lord.

ROMANS 8:38–39

Blessed be the God and Father of our Lord Jesus Christ, the Father of mercies and God of all comfort, who comforts us in all our tribulation, that we may be able to comfort those who are in any trouble, with the comfort with which we ourselves are comforted by God.

2 CORINTHIANS 1:3–4

. . . according to the eternal purpose which He accomplished in Christ Jesus our Lord, in whom we have boldness and access with confidence through faith in Him.

EPHESIANS 3:11–12

Finally, my brethren, be strong in the Lord and in the power of His might.

EPHESIANS 6:10

For God has not given us a spirit of fear, but of power and of love and of a sound mind.

2 TIMOTHY 1:7

Let us draw near with a true heart in full assurance of faith, having our hearts sprinkled from an evil conscience and our bodies washed with pure water.

HEBREWS 10:22

"So we may boldly say:
'The LORD is my helper;
I will not fear.
What can man do to me?'"

HEBREWS 13:6

And by this we know that we are of the truth, and shall assure our hearts before Him. For if our heart condemns us, God is greater than our heart, and knows all things. Beloved, if our heart does not condemn us, we have confidence toward God.

1 JOHN 3:19–21

FOR DISCOVERING THE HOLINESS GOD REQUIRES

For I am the LORD your God. You shall therefore consecrate yourselves, and you shall be holy; for I am holy. Neither shall you defile yourselves with any creeping thing that creeps on the earth.

LEVITICUS 11:44

"No one is holy like the LORD,
For there is none besides You,
Nor is there any rock like our God."

1 SAMUEL 2:2

"Oh, worship the LORD in the beauty of holiness!
Tremble before Him, all the earth."

PSALM 96:9

"How can a young man cleanse his way?
By taking heed according to Your word."

PSALM 119:9

"The fear of the LORD is the beginning of wisdom,
And the knowledge of the Holy One is understanding."

PROVERBS 9:10

"A highway shall be there, and a road,
And it shall be called the Highway of Holiness.
The unclean shall not pass over it,
But it shall be for others.
Whoever walks the road, although a fool,
Shall not go astray."

ISAIAH 35:8

"Thus I will magnify Myself and sanctify Myself, and I will be known in the eyes of many nations. Then they shall know that I am the LORD."

EZEKIEL 38:23

. . . in holiness and righteousness before Him all the days of our life.

LUKE 1:75

I speak in human terms because of the weakness of your flesh. For just as you presented your members as slaves of uncleanness, and of lawlessness leading to more lawlessness, so now present your members as slaves of righteousness for holiness.

ROMANS 6:19

For if the firstfruit is holy, the lump is also holy; and if the root is holy, so are the branches.

ROMANS 11:16

Therefore, having these promises, beloved, let us cleanse ourselves from all filthiness of the flesh and spirit, perfecting holiness in the fear of God.

2 CORINTHIANS 7:1

And those who are Christ's have crucified the flesh with its passions and desires. If we live in the Spirit, let us also walk in the Spirit.

GALATIANS 5:24–25

. . . just as He chose us in Him before the foundation of the world, that we should be holy and without blame before Him in love.

EPHESIANS 1:4

And may the Lord make you increase and abound in love
to one another and to all, just as we do to you, so that He may
establish your hearts blameless in holiness before our God and
Father at the coming of our Lord Jesus Christ with all His saints.

1 THESSALONIANS 3:12–13

For this is the will of God, your sanctification: that you
should abstain from sexual immorality; that each of you
should know how to possess his own vessel in sanctification
and honor.

1 THESSALONIANS 4:3–4

For God did not call us to uncleanness, but in holiness.

1 THESSALONIANS 4:7

Now may the God of peace Himself sanctify you
completely; and may your whole spirit, soul, and body be pre-
served blameless at the coming of our Lord Jesus Christ.

1 THESSALONIANS 5:23

[He] has saved us and called us with a holy calling, not
according to our works, but according to His own purpose and
grace which was given to us in Christ Jesus before time began.

2 TIMOTHY 1:9

Therefore if anyone cleanses himself from the latter, he will be a vessel for honor, sanctified and useful for the Master, prepared for every good work.

2 Timothy 2:21

For they indeed for a few days chastened us as seemed best to them, but He for our profit, that we may be partakers of His holiness.

Hebrews 12:10

Pursue peace with all people, and holiness, without which no one will see the Lord.

Hebrews 12:14

. . . as obedient children, not conforming yourselves to the former lusts, as in your ignorance; but as He who called you is holy, you also be holy in all your conduct, because it is written, "Be holy, for I am holy."

1 Peter 1:14–16

But you are a chosen generation, a royal priesthood, a holy nation, His own special people, that you may proclaim the praises of Him who called you out of darkness into His marvelous light.

1 PETER 2:9

FOR EXPERIENCING GOD'S MERCY AND LOVE

And He will love you and bless you and multiply you; He will also bless the fruit of your womb and the fruit of your land, your grain and your new wine and your oil, the increase of your cattle and the offspring of your flock, in the land of which He swore to your fathers to give you.

DEUTERONOMY 7:13

"Remember, O LORD, Your tender mercies and Your
    lovingkindnesses,
For they are from of old.
Do not remember the sins of my youth, nor my
    transgressions;
According to Your mercy remember me,
For Your goodness' sake, O LORD."

PSALM 25:6–7

"The LORD is merciful and gracious,
Slow to anger, and abounding in mercy."

PSALM 103:8

"The LORD is good to all,
And His tender mercies are over all His works."

PSALM 145:9

"But the mercy of the LORD is from everlasting to everlasting
On those who fear Him,
And His righteousness to children's children."

PSALM 103:17

"He who covers his sins will not prosper,
But whoever confesses and forsakes them will have mercy."

PROVERBS 28:13

"Therefore the LORD will wait, that He may be gracious
   to you;
And therefore He will be exalted, that He may have mercy
   on you.
For the LORD is a God of justice;
Blessed are all those who wait for Him."

ISAIAH 30:18

"The LORD has appeared of old to me, saying:
'Yes, I have loved you with an everlasting love;
Therefore with lovingkindness I have drawn you.'"

JEREMIAH 31:3

"Who is a God like You,
Pardoning iniquity
And passing over the transgression of the remnant of His
heritage?

He does not retain His anger forever,
Because He delights in mercy."

MICAH 7:18

"But go and learn what this means: 'I desire mercy and
not sacrifice.' For I did not come to call the righteous, but
sinners, to repentance."

MATTHEW 9:13

"And His mercy is on those who fear Him
From generation to generation."

LUKE 1:50

So he answered and said, "'You shall love the LORD your God with all your heart, with all your soul, with all your strength, and with all your mind,' and 'your neighbor as yourself.'"

LUKE 10:27

"And I have declared to them Your name, and will declare it, that the love with which You loved Me may be in them, and I in them."

JOHN 17:26

I beseech you therefore, brethren, by the mercies of God, that you present your bodies a living sacrifice, holy, acceptable to God, which is your reasonable service.

ROMANS 12:1

No temptation has overtaken you except such as is common to man; but God is faithful, who will not allow you to be tempted beyond what you are able, but with the temptation will also make the way of escape, that you may be able to bear it.

1 CORINTHIANS 10:13

And God is able to make all grace abound toward you, that you, always having all sufficiency in all things, may have an abundance for every good work.

2 CORINTHIANS 9:8

But God, who is rich in mercy, because of His great love with which He loved us, even when we were dead in trespasses, made us alive together with Christ (by grace you have been saved), and raised us up together, and made us sit together in the heavenly places in Christ Jesus.

EPHESIANS 2:4–6

Let us therefore come boldly to the throne of grace, that we may obtain mercy and find grace to help in time of need.

HEBREWS 4:16

For judgment is without mercy to the one who has shown no mercy. Mercy triumphs over judgment.

JAMES 2:13

FOR REVIVAL AND SPIRITUAL AWAKENING

If My people who are called by My name will humble themselves, and pray and seek My face, and turn

116

from their wicked ways, then I will hear from heaven, and will forgive their sin and heal their land.

2 CHRONICLES 7:14

"For if you return to the LORD, your brethren and your children will be treated with compassion by those who lead them captive, so that they may come back to this land; for the LORD your God is gracious and merciful, and will not turn His face from you if you return to Him."

2 CHRONICLES 30:9

"I have called upon You, for You will hear me, O God;
Incline Your ear to me, and hear my speech.
Show Your marvelous lovingkindness by Your right hand,
O You who save those who trust in You
From those who rise up against them.
Keep me as the apple of Your eye;
Hide me under the shadow of Your wings,
From the wicked who oppress me,
From my deadly enemies who surround me."

PSALM 17:6–9

"Will You not revive us again,
That Your people may rejoice in You?
Show us Your mercy, LORD,
And grant us Your salvation."

PSALM 85:6–7

"He shall call upon Me, and I will answer him;
I will be with him in trouble;
I will deliver him and honor him."

PSALM 91:15

"Oh, that You would rend the heavens!
That You would come down!
That the mountains might shake at Your presence."

ISAIAH 64:1

And I will give you shepherds according to My heart, who
will feed you with knowledge and understanding.

JEREMIAH 3:15

"Return, you backsliding children,
And I will heal your backslidings."

"Indeed we do come to You,
For You are the LORD our God."

JEREMIAH 3:22

But this is what I commanded them, saying, "Obey My voice, and I will be your God, and you shall be My people. And walk in all the ways that I have commanded you, that it may be well with you."

JEREMIAH 7:23

Then you will call upon Me and go and pray to Me, and I will listen to you.

JEREMIAH 29:12

"I will bring the one-third through the fire,
Will refine them as silver is refined,
And test them as gold is tested.
They will call on My name,
And I will answer them.
I will say, 'This is My people';
And each one will say, 'The LORD is my God.'"

ZECHARIAH 13:9

"I will seek what was lost and bring back what was driven away, bind up the broken and strengthen what was sick; but I will destroy the fat and the strong, and feed them in judgment."

EZEKIEL 34:16

I will give you a new heart and put a new spirit within you; I will take the heart of stone out of your flesh and give you a heart of flesh. I will put My Spirit within you and cause you to walk in My statutes, and you will keep My judgments and do them. Then you shall dwell in the land that I gave to your fathers; you shall be My people, and I will be your God.

EZEKIEL 36:26–28

"I will return again to My place
Till they acknowledge their offense.
Then they will seek My face;
In their affliction they will earnestly seek Me."

HOSEA 5:15

Praying the Scriptures

Therefore I say to you, whatever things you ask when you pray, believe that you receive them, and you will have them.

MARK 11:24

Now to Him who is able to do exceedingly abundantly above all that we ask or think, according to the power that works in us,

EPHESIANS 3:20

Therefore I exhort first of all that supplications, prayers, intercessions, and giving of thanks be made for all men, for kings and all who are in authority, that we may lead a quiet and peaceable life in all godliness and reverence. For this is good and acceptable in the sight of God our Savior, who desires all men to be saved and to come to the knowledge of the truth.

1 TIMOTHY 2:1–4

Let us therefore come boldly to the throne of grace, that we may obtain mercy and find grace to help in time of need.

HEBREWS 4:16

"For the eyes of the LORD are on the righteous,
And His ears are open to their prayers;
But the face of the LORD is against those who do evil."

1 PETER 3:12

If we confess our sins, He is faithful and just to forgive us our sins and to cleanse us from all unrighteousness.

1 JOHN 1:9

ACKNOWLEDGMENTS

To HarperCollins Christian Publishers
for asking us to share messages that have been so
meaningful to us and so impactful to God's people

and

Kerry Skinner who helped with the original
version of this book, and Richard Blackaby, who
made a major contribution to the revised edition.

ABOUT THE AUTHORS

Henry Blackaby has spent his life in ministry and holds five honorary doctorate degrees. He served as a pastor in California and Canada, was a Bible college president, and later served as a special assistant to the presidents of the North American Mission Board, the International Mission Board, and LifeWay Christian Resources. He is the founder and president emeritus of Blackaby Ministries International. Henry is also the author of dozens of books, including the Christian classic, *Experiencing God*. His titles have been translated into more than forty languages. He has spoken in more than 115 countries as well as the White House, the Pentagon, and the United Nations. He has mentored numerous CEOs of *Fortune* 500 companies and has been used powerfully by God to inspire churches, denominations, and Christian organizations to return to God in revival. Dr. Blackaby and his wife, Marilyn, have five married children, all serving in Christian ministry.

About the Authors

RICHARD BLACKABY IS HENRY'S OLDEST CHILD. HE IS THE president of Blackaby Ministries International (www .blackaby.org) and an international speaker on spiritual leadership, God in the marketplace, and experiencing God. He has written or coauthored dozens of books including *Experiencing God, Spiritual Leadership, Unlimiting God, Called to Be God's Leader, The Seasons of God, Living Out of the Overflow, Flickering Lamps, Putting a Face on Grace*, and *Fresh Encounter*. Richard lives in Atlanta with his wife, Lisa.